SECOND EDITION

# 3

# INSIDE READING

The Academic Word List in Context

Bruce Rubin

SERIES DIRECTOR:
**Cheryl Boyd Zimmerman**

**OXFORD**
UNIVERSITY PRESS

**OXFORD**
UNIVERSITY PRESS

198 Madison Avenue
New York, NY 10016 USA

Great Clarendon Street, Oxford, OX2 6DP, United Kingdom

Oxford University Press is a department of the University of Oxford.
It furthers the University's objective of excellence in research, scholarship,
and education by publishing worldwide. Oxford is a registered trade
mark of Oxford University Press in the UK and in certain other countries

General Manager, American ELT: Laura Pearson
Publisher: Stephanie Karras
Associate Publishing Manager: Sharon Sargent
Development Editor: Keyana Shaw
Director, ADP: Susan Sanguily
Executive Design Manager: Maj-Britt Hagsted
Electronic Production Manager: Julie Armstrong
Senior Designer: Yin Ling Wong
Designer: Jessica Balaschak
Image Manager: Trisha Masterson
Production Coordinator: Brad Tucker

ISBN: 978 0 19 441629 0 STUDENT BOOK

Printed in China

This book is printed on paper from certified and well-managed sources

ACKNOWLEDGEMENTS

*The authors and publisher are grateful to those who have given permission to reproduce
the following extracts and adaptations of copyright material:*

*Illustrations by*: p. 51 Infomen (infant); p. 51 Infomen (water); p. 52 Infomen; p.
60 Infomen; p. 83 Infomen; p. 105 Infomen; p. 156 Infomen (presentation); p.
156 Infomen (flow-chart); p. 156 Infomen (nurse); p. 156 Infomen (line-graph);
p. 156 Infomen (eye-chart); p. 156 Infomen (pie-chart).

*We would also like to thank the following for permission to reproduce the following
photographs*: Cover: Classic Image/Alamy (Acropolis); Lee Foster/Alamy (spices);
Bettmann/Corbis UK Ltd (Ferris Wheel); Dartfish ltd - Video Software Solutions
(skiers); Nikada/Getty Images (skyscraper); LdF/iStockphoto (compass);
Marilyn Volan/Shutterstock (diamonds); Inside front cover: Rstem Grler/
iStockphoto (iMac); Stephen Krow/iStockphoto (iPhone); pg. xii, Marcin
Krygier / iStockphoto (laptop); p. 1 Marilyn Volan/Shutterstock (background);
p. 1 Lee Foster/Alamy (spice); p. 3 Shaun Higson colour/Alamy; p. 4 sarra22/
Shutterstock; p. 11 Guy Gillette/Time & Life Pictures/Getty Images; p. 17
iStockphoto; p. 19 Data courtesy Marc Imhoff of NASA GSFC and Christopher
Elvidge of NOAA NGDC. Image by Craig Mayhew and Robert Simmon,
NASA GSFC/NASA (USA); p. 19 Data courtesy Marc Imhoff of NASA GSFC and
Christopher Elvidge of NOAA NGDC. Image by Craig Mayhew and Robert
Simmon, NASA GSFC/NASA (Japan); p. 26 Duncan Chard/Bloomberg/Getty
Images; p. 33 Bruno De Hogues/Sygma/Corbis UK Ltd.; p. 35 Janet Echelman/
Christina O'Haver/Studio Echelman, Inc.; p. 36 Carolyn Clarke/Alamy; p. 43
Claire Greenway/Getty Images; p. 49 jang14/Shutterstock; p. 65 James Balog/
Getty Images; p. 66 Dartfish ltd - Video Software Solutions; p. 67 Dartfish
ltd - Video Software Solutions; p. 73 Eadweard Muybridge//Time Life Pictures/
Getty Images; p. 74 Sami Sarkis Studio/Alamy; p. 81 David Wall/Alamy; p. 82
Bettmann/Corbis UK Ltd.; p. 88 JORDI CAMI/Alamy; p. 91 David Wall/Alamy;
p97 Corbis / Digital Stock/Oxford University Press; p100 Corbis / Digital
Stock/Oxford University Press; p113 bitt24/Shutterstock; p. 114 Stockbyte/
Thinkstock; p. 121 NickS/iStockphoto; p. 129 ra3rn/Shutterstock; p. 130 PCN

Photography/Alamy; p. 131 Picture Press/Alamy; p. 132 LIU, CHIN-CHENG/
Shutterstock; p. 138 Jeff Morgan 03/Alamy; p. 145 Ivan Mateev/iStockphoto;
p. 147 kaczor58/Shutterstock; p. 154 Alistair Scott/Alamy; p. 155 iStockphoto/
Thinkstock.

*The publisher would like to thank the following for their permission to reproduce the
following extracts and adaptations of material. Every effort was made to contact the
rights holders of extracted and adapted material. Please contact the publisher regarding
any rights ownership queries*: p. 18 Adapted from "The New Megalopolis," by
Richard Florida, Newsweek International Edition, July 3, 2006. Reprinted
by permission of the author; p. 25 Adapted from "Ecopolis Now" by Fred
Pearce, New Scientist, Vol. 190 Issue 2556, June 17, 2006. Copyright 2006
Reed Business Information–UK. All Rights Reserved. Distributed by Tribune
Media Services. Reprinted by permission; p. 36 Adapted from "Art Attack" by
Roxana Popescu, The Daily Beast, Dec. 27, 2007. Reprinted by permission of
the author; p. 43 "One Person's Vandalism is Another One's Art" by Lenore
Costello, Gotham Gazette, March 25, 2008. Copyright by and reprinted with
permission from Gotham Gazette (www.gothamgazette.com), a publication
on New York policy and politics; p. 51 Figure "World Infant Mortality Rates,
1950-2005." Source: Vital Signs 2006-2007 @ Worldwatch Institute, www.
worldwatch.org. Reprinted by permission of the Worldwatch Institute;  p. 51
Table 2 Effect of Filtration and Chlorination on Mortality, from "Chlorination,
Clean Water, and the Public Health Progress that Changed America,"
waterandhealth.org. Reprinted by permission of the American Chemistry
Council; p. 51 Based on information presented in "The Determinants of
Mortality," by David Cutler, Angus Deaton, and Adriana Lleras-Muney, Journal
of Economic Perspectives, Vol. 20, No. 3 Summer 2006. Used with permission;
p. 57 Adapted from "The Benefits of Immunization," http:///www.wpro.
who.int/exeres/CEF3E8A4-D201-4E04-A3BD-E4BEB81D7D74.htm. Reprinted
courtesy of the World Health Organization; p. 58 "Vaccine-Preventable
Diseases" figure, http://www.who.int/immunization_monitoring/diseases/en.
Reprinted courtesy of the World Health Organization; p. 58 Tables: "Annual
deaths in 2002 from vaccine-preventable diseases" and "Annual deaths in 2002
from diseases for which vaccines will be available soon" adapted from http://
www.who.int/immunization_monitoring/burden/estimates_burden/en/index.
html. Reprinted courtesy of the World Health Organization; p. 67 Adapted
from "BBC Sport uses StroMotion technique for first time in UK," BBC Press
Release, January 2006. Reprinted by permission of BBC Vision; p. 99 Adapted
from "This is Your Brain on Drugs," by Jonathan Weiner. From The New York
Times, 5/9/2004 © 2004 The New York Times. All rights reserved. Used by
permission and protected by the Copyright Laws of the United States. The
printing, copying, redistribution, or retransmission of this Content without
express written permission is prohibited; p. 105 Adapted from "Out-of-Body
Experience? Your Brain is to Blame" by Sandra Blakeslee, From The New York
Times, October 3, 2006 © 2006 The New York Times. All rights reserved. Used
by permission and protected by the Copyright Laws of the United States. The
printing, copying, redistribution, or retransmission of this Content without
express written permission is prohibited; p. 121 Adapted from "How to Raise a
Genius" by Nicholas Weinstock, The New York Times, April 8, 2001. Reprinted
by permission of Nicholas Weinstock; p. 147 Adapted from "Getting There:
The Science of Driving Directions," by Nick Paumgarten. Originally published
in The New Yorker, April 24, 2006.  Reprinted by permission; © 2006 Nick
Paumgarten. All rights reserved.

# Acknowledgements

*We would like to acknowledge the following individuals for their input during the development of the series:*

**Amina Saif Mohammed Al Hashamia**
College of Applied Sciences – Nizwa, Oman

**Amal Al Muqarshi**
College of Applied Sciences – Ibri, Oman

**Dr. Gail Al-Hafidh**
Sharjah Women's College –
Higher Colleges of Technology, U.A.E.

**Saleh Khalfan Issa Al-Rahbi**
College of Applied Sciences – Nizwa, Oman

**Chris Alexis**
College of Applied Sciences – Sur, Oman

**Bernadette Anayah**
Folsom Lake College, CA, U.S.A.

**Paul Blomeyer**
King Fahd Naval Academy, Jubail,
Kingdom of Saudi Arabia

**Judith Buckman**
College of Applied Sciences – Salalah, Oman

**Peter Bull**
Abu Dhabi Men's College –
Higher Colleges of Technology, U.A.E.

**Bjorn Candel**
Fujairah Men's College –
Higher Colleges of Technology, U.A.E

**Geraldine Chell**
Sharjah Women's College –
Higher Colleges of Technology, U.A.E

**Hui-chen Chen**
Shi-lin High School of Commerce, Taipei

**Kim Dammers**
Golden Bridge Educational Centre, Mongolia

**Steven John Donald**
Waikato Institute of Education, New Zealand

**Patricia Gairaud**
San Jose City College, CA, U.S.A.

**Joyce Gatto**
College of Lake County, IL, U.S.A.

**Sally Gearhart**
Santa Rosa Junior College, CA, U.S.A.

**Dr. Simon Green**
Colleges of Applied Sciences, Oman

**Andrew Hirst**
Sharjah Women's College –
Higher Colleges of Technology, U.A.E

**Elena Hopkins**
Delaware County Community College, DE, U.S.A.

**William Hussain**
College of Applied Sciences – Sur, Oman

**Tom Johnson**
Abu Dhabi Men's College –
Higher Colleges of Technology, U.A.E.

**Sei-Hwa Jung**
Catholic University of Korea, South Korea

**Graham Martindale**
SHCT Sharjah Higher –
Colleges of Technology, U.A.E.

**Mary McKee**
Abu Dhabi Men's College –
Higher Colleges of Technology, U.A.E.

**Lisa McMurray**
Abu Dhabi Men's College –
Higher Colleges of Technology, U.A.E.

**Sally McQuinn**
Fujairah Women's College –
Higher Colleges of Technology, U.A.E.

**Hsieh Meng-Tsung**
National Cheng Kung University, Tainan

**Marta Mueller**
Folsom Lake College, RCC, CA, U.S.A.

**Zekariya Özşevik**
Middle East Technical University, Turkey

**Margaret Plenert**
California State University, Fullerton UEE,
American Language Program, CA, U.S.A.

**Dorothy Ramsay**
College of Applied Sciences –
Sohar, Oman

**Cindy Roiland**
College of Lake County, IL, U.S.A.

**Elia Sarah**
State University of New York
at New Paltz, NY, U.S.A.

**Rachel Scott**
Sharjah Women's College –
Higher Colleges of Technology, U.A.E.

**Tony Sexton**
Abu Dhabi Men's College –
Higher Colleges of Technology, U.A.E.

**Siân Walters**
Sharjah Men's College –
Higher Colleges of Technology, U.A.E.

**Martin Weatherby**
St. Thomas University, Japan

# Contents

# An Insider's Guide to Academic Reading

Develop reading skills and acquire the Academic Word List with
*Inside Reading Second Edition.*

## Student Books

## iTools for all levels

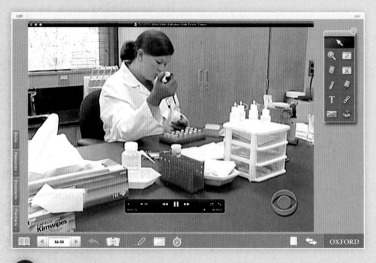

 Authentic video available on iTools and the Student Website.

# Getting Started

## Each unit in *Inside Reading* features

> **Two high-interest reading texts** from an academic content area

> **Reading skills** relevant to the academic classroom

> Targeted words from the **Academic Word List**

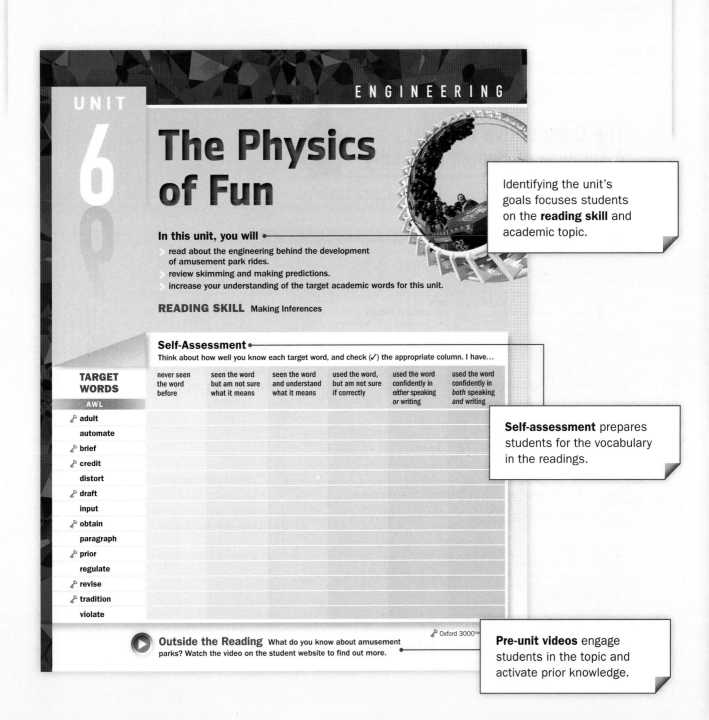

ENGINEERING

### UNIT 6

# The Physics of Fun

**In this unit, you will**
> read about the engineering behind the development of amusement park rides.
> review skimming and making predictions.
> increase your understanding of the target academic words for this unit.

**READING SKILL** Making Inferences

Identifying the unit's goals focuses students on the **reading skill** and academic topic.

### Self-Assessment

Think about how well you know each target word, and check (✓) the appropriate column. I have...

| TARGET WORDS | never seen the word before | seen the word but am not sure what it means | seen the word and understand what it means | used the word, but am not sure if correctly | used the word confidently in *either* speaking *or* writing | used the word confidently in *both* speaking *and* writing |
|---|---|---|---|---|---|---|
| **AWL** | | | | | | |
| 🔑 adult | | | | | | |
| automate | | | | | | |
| 🔑 brief | | | | | | |
| 🔑 credit | | | | | | |
| distort | | | | | | |
| 🔑 draft | | | | | | |
| input | | | | | | |
| 🔑 obtain | | | | | | |
| paragraph | | | | | | |
| 🔑 prior | | | | | | |
| regulate | | | | | | |
| 🔑 revise | | | | | | |
| 🔑 tradition | | | | | | |
| violate | | | | | | |

**Self-assessment** prepares students for the vocabulary in the readings.

**Outside the Reading** What do you know about amusement parks? Watch the video on the student website to find out more.

🔑 Oxford 3000™

**Pre-unit videos** engage students in the topic and activate prior knowledge.

# High-interest Texts

## READING 1

**Before You Read**

Read these questions. Discuss your answers in a small group.

1. Do you consider yourself to be a competitive person? Why or why not?
2. Do you think the urge to compete is something people are born with or something they learn from their parents? Why?
3. Does society have an effect on an individual's competitive drive? If so, how? Are some societies more competitive than others? Give examples to support your opinions.

**MORE WORDS YOU'LL NEED**

**instinct:** the natural force that causes a person or animal to behave in a certain way without thinking about it.

**Read**

This article is a timeline that traces the history of competition—personal, professional, and national.

## The Competitive Edge: A Timeline of Human Ingenuity

Are you a runner? A soccer player? Have you ever competed in a sport, felt the thrill of the game, or raced for the win? Why is it that our best performances are often those played against
5 our toughest competitors? Ask Liliya Shobukhova (top right) of Russia when she attained her best marathon time. She won't tell you she did it while training alone. She did it while running—and winning—the 2011 Chicago Marathon, her third
10 consecutive win. It's not just physical competition that inspires us. As many of us can testify, competition affects every aspect of life. The following timeline demonstrates that the competitive instinct has been around for a long
15 time and has produced some staggering results.

**ANCIENT HISTORY**
**THE STORIES WE TELL**
Before written language developed, oral stories were handed down from one generation to the

next. From Greek mythology to the plays of Shakespeare, **classical** literature abounds with
20 tales of rivalry between siblings. Often birth order, gender, and status within the family play into the clashes as siblings determine the best strategy for succeeding over the other. Whether it's for parental approval, wealth, or love, competition
25 between siblings is an age-old story. It's a drama we don't tire of easily.

**1206**
**THE LARGEST EMPIRE**
A boy abandoned in the Mongolian grasslands with his mother and siblings later controls the largest empire in history. As a warrior, he
30 conquers the tribes competing for control of Mongolia and brings them under his rule, thereby earning the title "Genghis Khan," which means "ruler of all between the oceans." Now acknowledged as a leader, he **commences**

130  UNIT 9

## Reading Comprehension

Read each sentence below. Choose the best answer to complete the sentence based on Reading 1.

1. According to the section "The Stories We Tell," humans have a long history of telling stories about _____.
   a. physical competition of athletes
   b. the path to literacy
   c. competition between siblings
2. Using rhymes to help soldiers remember and follow through on orders was a strategy _____ used.
   a. Filippo Brunelleschi
   b. Genghis Khan
   c. Prince Henry the Navigator
3. Capitalism is associated with competition because _____.
   a. businesses are allowed to compete
   b. William Makepeace Thackeray used the term
   c. it leads to better quality and lower prices

**Discussion questions activate students' knowledge** and prepare them to read.

**High-interest readings** motivate students.

**Academic Word List vocabulary** is presented in context.

**Comprehension activities** help students understand the text and apply the targeted academic vocabulary.

# Explicit Reading Skill Instruction

**READING SKILL** Summarizing a Text Using Nontext Elements

**LEARN**

The task of summarizing a text can be broken down into two steps:
- Figure out the central ideas of a selection.
- Combine them briefly and clearly.

Also be sure to include the nontext elements—such as pictures, tables, charts, and graphs—in your summary.

**APPLY**

1. Identify two main ideas in *The Dartfish Olympics*.

2. Identify two main ideas in *BBC Sport Uses StroMotion™ Technique*.

3. Look at the photos that accompany Reading 1. How do they link to the main ideas? Consider the photos on their own. What main idea do they present?

4. Combine the main ideas from 1, 2, and 3 above into a summary of Reading 1. One or two sentences should be enough.

> **Explicit reading skills** provide the foundation for effective, critical reading.

> **Practice exercises** enable students to implement new reading skills successfully.

**READING SKILL** Summarizing a Text Using Nontext Elements

**APPLY**

1. Identify two main topics in Reading 2.

2. Look at the photos that accompany Reading 2. How do they link to the main ideas? Consider the photos as a group. What main idea does the group present?

3. Combine the main ideas from the text and the accompanying images into a summary of Reading 2.

**REVIEW A SKILL** Identifying Main Ideas vs. Supporting Details (See p. 20)

Reread the article on pages 73–75. As you read each paragraph, think about the author's main purpose. Identify the main ideas and supporting details for each paragraph and write these in your notebook.

> **Recycling of reading skills** allows students to apply knowledge in new contexts.

# The Academic Word List in Context

Based on a corpus of 3.4 million words, the **Academic Word List (AWL)** is the most principled and widely accepted list of academic words. Compiled by Averil Coxhead in 2000, it was informed by academic materials across the academic disciplines.

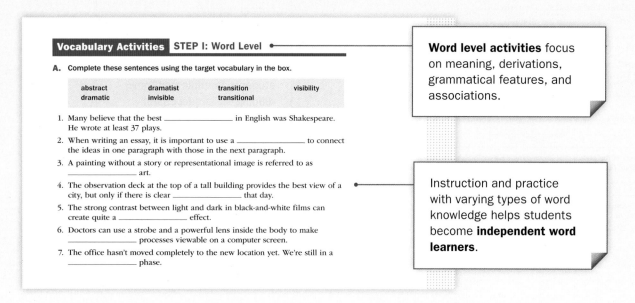

**Vocabulary Activities** STEP I: Word Level

**A.** Complete these sentences using the target vocabulary in the box.

| abstract | dramatist | transition | visibility |
|----------|-----------|------------|------------|
| dramatic | invisible | transitional | |

1. Many believe that the best _____ in English was Shakespeare. He wrote at least 37 plays.
2. When writing an essay, it is important to use a _____ to connect the ideas in one paragraph with those in the next paragraph.
3. A painting without a story or representational image is referred to as _____ art.
4. The observation deck at the top of a tall building provides the best view of a city, but only if there is clear _____ that day.
5. The strong contrast between light and dark in black-and-white films can create quite a _____ effect.
6. Doctors can use a strobe and a powerful lens inside the body to make _____ processes viewable on a computer screen.
7. The office hasn't moved completely to the new location yet. We're still in a _____ phase.

> **Word level activities** focus on meaning, derivations, grammatical features, and associations.

> Instruction and practice with varying types of word knowledge helps students become **independent word learners**.

**Vocabulary Activities** STEP II: Sentence Level

An *image* has both concrete and abstract meanings, but they all connect to the idea of a picture of something.

> The **images** on the screen reminded him of the town where he grew up.
> The **image** of the building was beautifully reflected in the lake.
> Many people have the **image** of Canada as being cold all the time.
> Ads try to create a positive **image** of a product.

The verb *imagine* and the noun *imagination* also come from the word *image*.

There are many expressions and collocations that feature the word *image*.

> She <u>is the very image of</u> her sister.     (She looks exactly like her sister.)
> He <u>is the very image of</u> sophistication.     (He has all the qualities of sophistication.)
> She <u>is the spitting image of</u> her father.     (She looks and acts like her father.)

CORPUS

> **Vocabulary work progresses** to sentence level and focuses on collocations, register, specific word usage, and learner dictionaries.

**E.** Match each use of the word *image* with the field to which it typically belongs. Then, write an example sentence for each context. Discuss your sentences in a small group.

___ 1. art          a. the public personality or character presented by a person

___ 2. psychology          b. a symbol or metaphor that represents something else

___ 3. business/marketing          c. a duplication of the visual form of a person or object

___ 4. literature          d. an advertising concept conveyed to the public

*Psychology: As role models for young people, pop stars should maintain a*
*healthy, responsible image.*

_____

_____

# From Research to Practice

The Oxford English Corpus provides **the most relevant and accurate picture of the English language.** It is based on a collection of over two billion carefully-selected and inclusive 21$^{st}$ century English texts.

The word *sphere* can refer to any round object or something having a round dynamic, like this instance from Reading 1:

*"…brains, software, cities, and ant heaps … become the webs and* **spheres** *of efficient mass circuitry."*

In Reading 2, *sphere* refers to "an area of interest or activity":

*"People often attribute such experiences to paranormal forces outside the* **sphere** *of material life."*

The related word *hemisphere* means "half of a sphere." In biology, it is used to refer to the left and right sides of the brain. In geography, it is used to refer to parts of the world.

*Most parts of the brain related to language are in the right* **hemisphere***.*

*In the northern* **hemisphere***, winter is in December, January, and February.*

CORPUS

> **Corpus-based** examples from the **Oxford English Corpus** of American English. Real-life examples help students learn authentic English.

**B.** Categorize these synonyms for *sphere* by definition. (One of the words will be used twice.) Add any other synonyms for *sphere* you can think of to the lists.

| ball | domain | globe | zone |
|------|--------|-------|------|
| circle | field | planet | |

| round | area of interest or activity |
|-------|------------------------------|
| _____ | _____ |
| _____ | _____ |
| _____ | _____ |
| _____ | _____ |

**C.** Complete these sentences using the words in the box. Compare answers with a partner.

| academic sphere | sphere of influence | wider sphere |
|-----------------|---------------------|--------------|
| hemispheres | spherical objects | |

1. Artists must be able to draw square, cylindrical, triangular, and _____ , like oranges and balls.
2. Historically, China has had a broad _____ in East Asia.
3. The globe can be divided into four _____ : Eastern, Western, Northern, and Southern.
4. The professor's work is little known outside the _____ of the university.
5. His books are detective stories, but he hopes that they will appeal to a _____ than only mystery lovers.

# Resources

## STUDENT SUPPORT

**For additional resources visit:**

www.oup.com/elt/student/insidereading

> **Reading worksheets** provide additional skill practice
> **Videos** set the stage for specific units
> **Audio recordings** of every reading text

## TEACHER SUPPORT

**The *Inside Reading* iTools is for use with an LCD projector or interactive whiteboard.**

### Resources for whole-class presentation

> Audio **recordings** of all **reading texts with "click and listen"** interactive scripts
> **Animated presentations** of reading skills for whole class presentations
> **Videos** for specific units introduce students to the reading text topic and activate prior knowledge.
> **Fun vocabulary activities** for whole-class participation

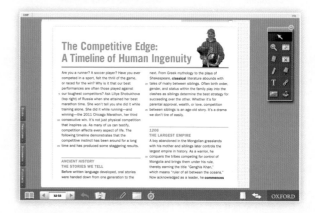

### Resources for assessment and preparation

> Printable worksheets for **extra reading skill practice**
> Printable and customizable **unit, mid-term, and final tests**
> Answer Keys
> Teaching Notes
> Video transcripts

**Additional resources at:**

www.oup.com/elt/teacher/insidereading

# UNIT 1

# From Market to Mall

## In this unit, you will

> read about the history of the shopping center and developments that led to the birth of the modern shopping mall.
> learn about the design and function of shopping centers.
> increase your understanding of the target academic words for this unit.

**READING SKILL** Previewing and Predicting

## Self-Assessment

Think about how well you know each target word, and check (✓) the appropriate column. I have…

| TARGET WORDS | never seen the word before | seen the word but am not sure what it means | seen the word and understand what it means | used the word, but am not sure if correctly | used the word confidently in *either* speaking *or* writing | used the word confidently in *both* speaking *and* writing |
|---|---|---|---|---|---|---|
| **AWL** | | | | | | |
| academy | | | | | | |
| 🔑 approach | | | | | | |
| 🔑 concept | | | | | | |
| 🔑 construct | | | | | | |
| 🔑 couple | | | | | | |
| enhance | | | | | | |
| 🔑 function | | | | | | |
| 🔑 partner | | | | | | |
| 🔑 pose | | | | | | |
| 🔑 publication | | | | | | |
| 🔑 range | | | | | | |
| 🔑 region | | | | | | |
| 🔑 select | | | | | | |
| simulate | | | | | | |
| 🔑 uniform | | | | | | |

🔑 Oxford 3000™ keywords

1

## Before You Read

**Read these questions. Discuss your answers in a small group.**

1. Describe your favorite shopping center or mall. What is special about it? What types of things do you usually buy there?

2. Besides shopping, what else is there to do at the mall? Are there things just for people your age? For young children? For older people?

3. Do you think that shopping malls are part of a community or something separate from it? Why? Do you think they've always been that way?

## READING SKILL | Previewing and Predicting

### LEARN

Previewing a text helps you predict what the text is going to be about. This helps prepare you for taking in information and remembering it.

Before reading a text, preview it:
- Read the titles or headlines.
- Look at the pictures and read the captions.
- Skim the text for names and details that are mentioned frequently.

This allows you to *anticipate the topic* of the text and prepare yourself to learn more about it.

### APPLY

**Skim Reading 1. Look for and note these things. Then make some predictions.**

1. A frequently mentioned location or type of building: _____

   _____

   _____

2. Some dates: _____

   _____

   _____

3. Some specific global locations: _____

   _____

   _____

4. Some information sources: _____

   _____

   _____

5. What is this text going to be about? _____

   _____

   _____

🔊 **Read**

This magazine article traces the history of shopping centers through various cultures.

# The Architecture of the Marketplace

**B**uildings are among the most lasting of human creations. Their forms and **functions** are evidence of the dynamic social life that has long been tied to centers of 5 economic and political power. One ancient structure and gathering place, the marketplace, has evolved into what we call today the **regional** shopping center or mall. It is often **constructed** on a site so big that it requires a 10 location outside of the crowded urban center. There it sometimes develops into a commercial rival to the older city center.

In many ways, these 21st-century malls are nothing new. In fact, they follow a long tradition 15 of commercial expansion that began with the development of the first long-distance trade networks and markets. These markets were temporary at first, but they became more permanent with the rise of cities in the Middle 20 East about five thousand years ago. They grew alongside the rivers, harbors, and overland caravan routes that connected the swelling towns of the agricultural era.

The population growth and economic 25 prosperity of the agricultural society made possible the advancement of specialized craftspeople and merchants. These people met to barter, buy, or sell their merchandise in a place that was accessible, safe, and regulated. By 30 2000 BC, in the ancient Sumerian city of Ur (in what is now Iraq), the covered bazaar and the shop-lined street had established itself.

The traditional bazaar consists of shops in streets that can be closed off by gates at each 35 end. This follows the historical town-planning requirement that commercial and residential areas be kept strictly apart. Though they are far from **uniform**, bazaars are typically divided into

A bazaar in Istanbul, Turkey

various sections that each specialize in a single 40 trade or craft. In small towns, the bazaar can be as small as a single covered street, while in large cities it can be a vast area filled with mazelike passageways. The Grand Bazaar of Tehran is ten kilometers long, while the one in Istanbul, 45 dating from the 15th century, has more than 58 streets and 4,000 shops. Historically, as in modern times, the bazaar was a source of tax revenue for the government. In return, the government provided the bazaars with a system 50 of internal security and justice.

In the Greek cities of the 5th century BC, the marketplace was the *agora*. The historian Lewis Mumford describes the agora as an open-air "place of assembly … where the interchange of 55 news and opinion played almost as important a part as the interchange of goods." The agora was also a place for seasonal festivals and sports such as horse racing. The expansion of the agora

in both physical size and variety of
60 traded goods reflected the shift in
the Greek economy from
neighborly rural trading to long-
distance multicultural exchange.
The descendants of the agora are
65 the piazzas and plazas in both
Europe and the Americas.

One of the most appealing
variations on the model of the
ancient marketplace was the
70 European arcade that appeared in
the 18th century. An arcade was
typically a covered set of city
streets similar to the bazaar, but it
retained some of the openness of
75 the agora through the use of
vaulted, or arched, skylights. One
of the first arcades was the Gostiny
Dvor in St. Petersburg, Russia, built
between 1757 and 1785. It has an open floor that
80 **simulates** the Italian piazza but is covered by a
glass roof that imitates the openness of the
agora even during cold Russian winters. The
Gostiny Dvor remains one of the finest shopping
centers in Northern Europe.

85 In Southern Europe, the Galleria Vittorio
Emanuele II, named after the first king of united
Italy, opened in Milan in 1867. Vaulted iron and
glass ceilings provide both shelter and light for
shopping in the middle of a dense city.

90 A young Viennese architect named Victor
Gruen was among the many visitors who were
favorably impressed by the Galleria. In the
1950s, Gruen was commissioned[1] to design a
**regional** shopping mall in the state of
95 Minnesota in the northern United States. The
Galleria Vittorio Emanuele II served as the
starting **concept** for his mall design.

The cold weather in Minnesota **posed** a
special challenge to shopper comfort. Gruen's
100 **approach** was to enclose the whole building.
The mall was built away from big cities and
was accessible mainly by automobile, so it
required a sea of automobile parking spaces
outside. The result, called Southdale, was a
105 spacious suburban destination. It attempted

A piazza in Zagreb, Croatia

to retain the inviting festivity of the agora,
the energy of the bazaar, and the lightness
of the arcade. It included **enhanced** climate
control, easy access, and a **range** of other
110 inviting conveniences and attractions.
Southdale soon became the archetype[2] for
the modern mall.

Since Southdale, huge **regional** shopping
malls have sprung up all over the world. They
115 commonly include several main "anchor" stores,
an ice skating rink, movie theaters, a themed
hotel, and an amusement park or other major
attraction. Such huge shopping and entertainment
centers depend on the willingness and ability of
120 people to travel some distance and shop or play
for long periods of time.

In the early 2000s, hundreds of such malls
were constructed in the People's Republic of
China. In 2008, a vast complex in the United
125 Arab Emirates, the Dubai Mall, attracted over
37 million visitors in its first year alone. The
mall, one of the largest in the world, features
over 1,200 stores, a marine aquarium, and an
Olympic-size ice skating rink. It is a magnet
130 for visitors, and its surrounding neighborhood
has been called "the new heart of the city."
Other world malls of note include the Istanbul
Cevahir, the Mall Taman Anggrek (Orchid

---

[1] *commissioned:* officially asked to make or create something
[2] *archetype:* the most typical or perfect example of a particular thing

Garden Mall) in Jakarta, Indonesia, and the
135 West Edmonton Mall in Alberta, Canada, which
features a water park.

From moveable markets, to bazaars and
agoras, to the sprawling modern **regional**

mall, the social function of a marketplace has
140 changed greatly. One thing remains the same:
these centers of trade and retail marketing
indicate economic prosperity and serve as
global status symbols. ■

## Reading Comprehension

Mark each sentence as *T* (true) or *F* (false) according to the information in Reading 1.
In your notebook, cite the location of the information by line number, and correct
each false statement.

___ 1. Regional shopping centers and malls exist today in a wide range of global
locations.

___ 2. The construction of a large retail center is an indication of economic
prosperity.

___ 3. The concept of a regional trade market is new to human social life.

___ 4. Agriculture created food surpluses that enhanced the development of
civilization.

___ 5. The open-air market called the *agora* originally came from South America.

___ 6. The bazaars of the Middle East are quite uniform in appearance.

___ 7. The European arcades simulated both the bazaar and the agora.

___ 8. Architect Victor Gruen's approach to Southdale, a fully enclosed American
shopping complex, was inspired by an arcade he had seen in Russia.

## Vocabulary Activities   STEP I: Word Level

The word *uniform*, as a noun, refers to the set of clothes worn by people in
the same job or organization, for example, a military uniform or a football
uniform.

As an adjective, *uniform* means "the same in all cases and at all times." It
is often used for technical descriptions, for example, uniform standards for
construction projects.

CORPUS

**A.** Which aspects of these things or situations should be uniform? Discuss your
answers in a small group. What else should be uniform or have uniform aspects?

1. a busy city street
2. chain restaurants
3. textbooks used in one school
4. schools in different regions

5. workers in the same company
6. cars
7. other: _____
8. other: _____

## Word Form Chart

| Noun | Verb | Adjective | Adverb |
|------|------|-----------|--------|
| pose | pose | posed | _____ |
| uniform | _____ | uniform | uniformly |
| construction | construct | constructive | constructively |
| simulation | simulate | simulated | _____ |
| enhancement | enhance | enhanced | _____ |
| region | _____ | regional | regionally |
| concept | conceptualize | conceptual | conceptually |

**B.** Using the target words in the chart, complete the sentences. Be sure to use the correct form and tense of each word.

1. _____ an aquarium and an ice-skating rink in a hot desert
   *(building)*
   climate _____ a special challenge to architects in the U.A.E.
   *(presented)*

2. The development of _____ trade markets _____
   *(area-wide)*                                      *(improved)*
   opportunities for specialized craftspeople and merchants.

3. Covering the streets of the bazaar was an _____ that dealt with
   *(improvement)*
   the need for climate control in the Middle East.

4. St. Petersburg's Gostiny Dvor was _____ in the 18th century but
   *(built)*
   remains one of the nicest shopping centers in the _____ today.
   *(area)*

5. A few malls in China _____ American amusement parks like
   *(pretend to be)*
   Disneyland in an effort to attract more shoppers.

**C.** Work with a partner. Write down at least one example of each type of region.
1. a geographic region: *the Middle East* _____
2. a metropolitan region: _____
3. an industrial region: _____
4. an agricultural region: _____
5. a region known for a specific feature or activity: _____

The word *academy* generally refers to a school for special instruction or training, as in an art academy, military academy, or tennis academy.

The adjective form, *academic*, refers to education in general—for example, this book focuses on the Academic Word List.

CORPUS

**D.** How important are these concepts to you? Why? Write a complete sentence for each. Consult your dictionary, if needed. Be prepared to discuss your ideas.

1. academic integrity _____

_____

_____

2. academic freedom _____

_____

_____

3. academic standards _____

_____

_____

4. academic community _____

_____

_____

**E.** Answer the questions in your notebook. Use at least one of the target academic words in each answer. Compare your sentences with a partner.

1. The ancient Greek agora was not only a marketplace, but also an arena for festivals and sports. Does the modern shopping mall continue this tradition in some way? How so?

2. In what ways does the modern mall resemble the Persian bazaar? How do malls maintain Islamic town planning requirements?

3. If Victor Gruen had stayed in Europe or immigrated to a different country, do you think he would have invented the mall there? Why or why not?

4. Is shopping at a mall different from shopping in a typical downtown environment? Why or why not?

5. What are some factors that are fundamental to the design of a shopping mall? Why are they important? Which ones originated with the European arcade?

The word *pose* has two verb forms. The first form is *intransitive*—it does not take an object. It means either "to sit for a portrait" or "to pretend to be other than what one is."

> Sometimes people don't like to **pose** for photos.

> The reporter **posed** as a sick person to investigate the hospital.

The second form is *transitive*—it must have an object. It means "to present, raise, put forward, bring up, or propose something."

> The extreme cold of Russian winters **posed** <u>a challenge</u> to the arcade designers in St. Petersburg. The very hot climate of Dubai **posed** <u>a challenge</u> to mall designers there.

CORPUS

**F.** Think of things that pose questions or concerns for you, your region, or for the planet in general. Write complete sentences and be prepared to explain your ideas to your classmates.

1. Something that poses a concern

   For you: _____

   For your region: _____

   For our planet: _____

2. Something that poses an opportunity

   For you: _____

   For your region: _____

   For our planet: _____

3. Something that poses a challenge

   For you: _____

   For your region: _____

   For our planet: _____

4. Something that poses a threat

   For you: _____

   For your region: _____

   For our planet: _____

5. Something that poses a difficult choice, or *dilemma*

   For you: _____

   For your region: _____

   For our planet: _____

## Before You Read

Read these questions. Discuss your answers in a small group.

1. What is the function of a press release? Who is the audience?

2. What information do you think should be in a press release? What information should not be in it?

3. Think about the first reading in this unit. Do you think the publicity for Southdale Mall was successful? Why or why not? How do you know?

## READING SKILL  Previewing and Predicting

### LEARN

As you preview a text for the general topic, you should also think about the focus of it.

First, preview the reading:
- Read the titles or headlines.
- Look at the pictures and read the captions.
- Skim the text for names and details that are mentioned frequently.

Then, ask yourself these questions:
- How is the reading organized?
- Who is the audience?
- What is the writer trying to accomplish?

Understanding the focus of the text will help you understand the writer's purpose for it.

### APPLY

Preview Reading 2 and answer these questions. After you've read the text, come back to check your answers.

1. What is the text about? _____

2. Who wrote this text? _____

3. What is the purpose of the text? _____

4. How does the focus differ from Reading 1? _____

This is a typical press release. It was one of several announcing the opening of the
Southdale Mall. Southdale was the prototype of the modern, fully enclosed, multilevel
shopping center that has spread around the world.

# PRESS RELEASE

FOR RELEASE: October 7, 1956

FROM: Harry Levine,
       Ruder & Finn, Incorporated
       130 East 59 Street
       New York, 22, New York, Plaza 9-1800

FOR: DAYTON'S SOUTHDALE CENTER, THE ARCHITECTS OF SOUTHDALE

### I. VICTOR GRUEN & ASSOCIATES

Victor Gruen & Associates is a planning team
of architects and engineers with headquarters in
Los Angeles and offices in Detroit, New York,
5 Minneapolis, and San Francisco.

Actively engaged in projects in almost every
state as well as abroad, the Gruen organization
was chosen as architect for Southdale in 1952.

The five **partners** of the firm, Victor Gruen,
10 Karl Van Leuven, Jr., R. L. Baumfeld, Edgardo
Contini, and Ben S. Southland, were brought
together in the common belief that individual
ingenuity **coupled** with disciplined teamwork
offers the best **approach** to today's complex
15 problems in planning.

As senior **partner**, Victor Gruen is
responsible for the **concept** development of
major projects. R. L. Baumfeld heads the Los
Angeles office and has been in charge of many
20 large projects, among them the Southdale Center.
Edgardo Contini directs engineering for the firm
and is in charge of coordinating engineering and
architectural design. Karl Van Leuven, Jr., head of
the Detroit office, has been the **partner** in charge
25 of such major projects as Northland **Regional**
Shopping Center in Detroit. Ben S. Southland is
chief designer and director of planning.

Herman Guttman, project coordinator for the
Southdale Shopping Center, is head of the Victor

30 Gruen Minneapolis office and is an associate in
the firm.

Victor Gruen & Associates has steadily
expanded the **range** of its activities. In the
commercial field, the firm has progressed from
35 the planning of individual shops and department
stores to the development of planned **regional**
shopping centers that have changed American
shopping habits.

In the residential field, Victor Gruen &
40 Associates has planned everything from
individual houses, apartments, and housing
projects to complete community developments
that meet all the needs of modern living.

Among Gruen projects of special interest are:
45 Milliron's Department Store (now The
Broadway) in Los Angeles, the first one-story
department store with roof parking.

The Mid-Wilshire Medical Building and two
13-story Tishman Buildings in Los Angeles, all
50 representing advances in design and planning
(lightweight steel buildings).

A number of large **regional** shopping
centers throughout the country, among them
Northland in Detroit, the world's largest. Others
55 include Eastland, also in suburban Detroit,
Glendale in Indianapolis, Valley Fair and
Bay Fair, both in the San Francisco Bay area,
and South Bay in Redondo Beach, California.

(The latter in association with Quincy Jones and Frederick Emmons, Architects A.I.A.).

Master planning for the Palos Verdes Peninsula, providing for residential, civic, commercial, educational, and recreational development of an outstanding land area of 7000 acres.

Master planning for the redevelopment of a downtown area in Detroit (the Gratiot-Orleans area), in association with Oskar Stonorov and Minoru Yamasaki.

A comprehensive study for redevelopment of the entire downtown area of Fort Worth, Texas. The study has produced a dramatic plan for renewal of the heart of the city through a long-**range** program aimed at solving traffic, parking, and urban rehabilitation problems.

The Gruen organization created the master plan for Southdale, in addition to designing the **regional** shopping center. In addition to Dayton's, it designed the following stores and special facilities:

Egekvist Bakery, Boutell's, Walters, the First National Bank, Thorpe Bros., J. B. Hudson Company, Juster Bros., Peter Pan Restaurant, Bringgold Meat Company, Bjorkman's, Sidewalk Café, Garner Records, The Children's Center, and The Toy Fair.

## II. VICTOR GRUEN

Victor Gruen, the head of Victor Gruen & Associates, was born in Vienna, Austria, where he received his architectural training at the Technological Institute, Advanced Division for Building **Construction**, and the **Academy** of Fine Arts. He was certified as an architect in Vienna in 1929 and practiced in that city until 1938, when he moved to the United States and opened his first office in New York. He is a registered architect in many states and his firm now has offices in Los Angeles, Detroit, New York, Minneapolis, and San Francisco.

Gruen's early work was in the fields of individual store design and residential projects. He is regarded as a pioneer in modern store design in work **ranging** from small shops to large department stores. Gruen turned to shopping center design early as a challenging

Southdale Mall in 1957

new field of architectural expression. He again won praise. As this firm expanded, the scope of his professional work grew to include such diverse projects as office buildings, private homes, public and tract housing projects, and the planning of complete communities including homes, apartment buildings, office buildings, shopping centers, civic buildings, schools, and recreational facilities. His unique achievements in these fields, especially in the design of shopping centers, have led him in recent years into the field of city planning and urban redevelopment.

Gruen's work has been widely published in such professional **publications** as PROGRESSIVE ARCHITECTURE and ARCHITECTURAL FORUM; in professional books such as SHOPS AND STORES and FORMS AND FUNCTIONS OF TWENTIETH CENTURY ARCHITECTURE; in technical and trade **publications** such as LIGHTING, ENGINEERING NEWS RECORD, THE AMERICAN CITY, and in FORTUNE, BUSINESS WEEK, THE SATURDAY EVENING POST, LIFE, THE NEW YORKER, COLLIER'S, LADIES HOME JOURNAL, McCALL'S, and HARVARD BUSINESS REVIEW.

He has spoken frequently before professional, technical, business, and planning groups and has written many articles for professional, trade, and business **publications**, and is presently working on two books. He has been **selected** for numerous awards for outstanding architectural work by the American Institute of Architects and other groups.

140    Of special interest is Gruen's comprehensive study of shopping center planning, written in collaboration with Lawrence P. Smith, which comprised the entire June 1952 issue of PROGRESSIVE ARCHITECTURE; and a traveling

145 exhibition, "The Shopping Center of Tomorrow," created for the American Federation of Arts and shown in leading museums throughout the United States and abroad. ■

## Reading Comprehension

Mark each sentence as *T* (true) or *F* (false) according to the information in Reading 2.

___ 1. Victor Gruen's firm consists only of architects.

___ 2. The firm has designed both commercial and residential projects.

___ 3. As senior partner, Gruen is mainly responsible for developing project concepts.

___ 4. When they began construction on Southdale, Gruen and his partners had little experience designing shopping centers.

___ 5. Gruen and his partners designed not only the shopping center but also several of the stores and facilities inside the center.

___ 6. This firm has offices in several cities.

___ 7. Gruen's work is of little interest to other professional architects.

___ 8. According to the press release, the development of planned regional shopping centers has changed American shopping habits.

## Vocabulary Activities    STEP I: Word Level

**A.** Read these sentences about the development of the modern shopping center; then restate each one using the word(s) in parentheses. Do not change the meanings of the sentences. Discuss your changes with a partner or small group.

1. In his method of thinking about the Southdale design, Victor Gruen raised several important questions. (*approach, posed*)

2. How could a shopping center be improved and made more comfortable in all kinds of weather? (*enhanced*)

3. Why would customers choose a shopping center that might be far from home and beyond their usual travel distance? (*select, range*)

4. In developing his basic idea, Gruen also wondered what would cause customers to stay longer in the mall and buy a wider variety of things. (*concept, range*)

5. He decided that it was more important to combine the energy of the city with the order and cleanliness of the suburbs. (*couple*)

A *partner* is someone associated with another person in some way and for some purpose. There are many types of *partners*. Some partnerships are related to work and business, while others function on a more personal level. These can relate to school, family life, politics, or even crime.

CORPUS

**B.** Look up these words in your dictionary. What type of partnership does each one suggest? There may be more than one answer for some words. Compare answers with a partner. Can you think of any other types of partnerships?

1. accomplice: *crime* _____
2. ally: _____
3. associate: _____
4. collaborator: _____
5. colleague: _____
   Others: _____

6. co-worker: _____
7. roommate: _____
8. sidekick: _____
9. spouse: _____
10. teammate: _____

**C.** Match the different types of publications with their descriptions. Use a dictionary if necessary.

___ 1. book
___ 2. magazine
___ 3. journal
___ 4. newspaper
___ 5. brochure
___ 6. booklet
___ 7. catalog

a. a thin glossy pamphlet with pictures in it that gives information about a specific product or program

b. a large-sized daily (or weekly) publication focusing on current events

c. a hard-cover or paperback publication containing a continuous story or narrative

d. a small publication that usually goes with another item, for example, instructions for using a product

e. a soft-cover publication focusing on a specific area of interest, for example, fashion, cars, or a sport

f. a soft-cover publication listing a store's products or a school's courses

g. a soft-cover publication sponsored by an academic or professional society and focused on issues in that field

**D.** Use the names of the publications in activity C (in the correct form) to complete the sentences.

1. At the student center, you can pick up a _____ about study-abroad programs.

2. Most research libraries keep a range of _____ from different organizations. When you need to find an academic or scientific article, you should check those first.

3. Some people don't like to go to the mall. They might prefer to order the things they want from a store's _____ and have them sent to their home.

4. I want to read the latest _____ by my favorite author, but the hard-cover versions are so expensive. I usually wait until they come out in paperback.

5. Most video games come with an instruction _____ that explains how to play the game.

6. My father reads the _____ every morning because he wants to know what's happening in the world quickly. I prefer to read a weekly news _____ because it has enhanced coverage of current events along with some analysis.

## Vocabulary Activities  STEP II: Sentence Level

The context of a sentence can help you learn how to use a word correctly. For this reason, dictionaries often include sample sentences that give you clues about meaning, collocations (words that go together), and levels of formality.

**E.** Read the sample sentences in the box that feature the words *approach* and *range*. Then write a new sample sentence for each one, using *approach* or *range* in the same meaning and word form.

Summer is **approaching**.

The truck **approached** the bridge.

Her performance **approached** perfection.

She **approached** her boss for a raise.

She used a logical **approach** to solve the problem.

Some cars are out of his price **range**.

His singing voice has a broad **range**.

The students **ranged** in age from fifteen to twenty-five.

The buffalo once **ranged** across western North America.

Computer manufacturers offer a wide **range** of product choices.

CORPUS

1. *I have to buy him a present soon because his birthday is approaching.*
_____

2. _____
_____

3. _____
_____

4. _____
_____

5. _____
_____

6. _____
_____

7. _____
_____

8. _____
_____

9. _____
_____

10. _____
_____

**F.** **Think about a traditional approach to these universal activities. Summarize that approach briefly. Then imagine a non-traditional approach to the same behavior or activity and summarize that approach.**

1. Sports and athletics

   Traditional: *Athletes competed only for glory, not money, and only the young played sports.*

   Non-traditional: *Sporting events have become a major entertainment business; all ages play sports for exercise.*

2. Cooking and eating

   Traditional: _____
   _____

   Non-traditional: _____
   _____

3. Medicine and surgery

   Traditional: _____
   _____

   Non-traditional: _____
   _____

4. Studying and taking a test

Traditional: _____

_____

Non-traditional: _____

_____

5. Hygiene and body adornment

_____

Traditional: _____

_____

Non-traditional: _____

_____

6. Buying and selling goods

Traditional: _____

_____

Non-traditional: _____

_____

Choose one of the topics above and on a separate piece of paper write a paragraph describing the different approaches. Be prepared to present your ideas.

G. Self-Assessment Review: Go back to page 1 and reassess your knowledge of the target vocabulary. How has your understanding of the words changed? What words do you feel most comfortable with now?

## Writing and Discussion Topics

Write about or discuss the following topics.

1. How do you expect malls to change in the future? How would you enhance the mall of today to create the mall of the future?

2. What are the negative aspects of shopping malls and of shopping in malls? How are these negative aspects addressed in other shopping formats?

3. According to the 1956 press release (Reading 2), the development of planned regional shopping centers changed the traditional approach to shopping and traditional concepts of shopping. Do you think the Internet has had as big an impact on shopping habits as malls did—or bigger? Why or why not?

# UNIT 2

# Megacities

## In this unit, you will

> read about the development of cities and megacities—and what the future holds for urban life around the globe.
> review previewing and predicting a reading selection.
> increase your understanding of the target academic words for this unit.

**READING SKILL** Identifying Main Ideas vs. Supporting Details

## TARGET WORDS

**AWL**

- 🔑 communicate
- 🔑 define
- 🔑 despite
- extract
- globe
- 🔑 major
- migrate
- 🔑 network
- 🔑 perspective
- 🔑 rely
- 🔑 remove
- 🔑 source
- 🔑 status
- 🔑 survive

## Self-Assessment

Think about how well you know each target word, and check (✓) the appropriate column. I have…

| | never seen the word before | seen the word but am not sure what it means | seen the word and understand what it means | used the word, but am not sure if correctly | used the word confidently in *either* speaking *or* writing | used the word confidently in *both* speaking *and* writing |
|---|---|---|---|---|---|---|
| communicate | | | | | | |
| define | | | | | | |
| despite | | | | | | |
| extract | | | | | | |
| globe | | | | | | |
| major | | | | | | |
| migrate | | | | | | |
| network | | | | | | |
| perspective | | | | | | |
| rely | | | | | | |
| remove | | | | | | |
| source | | | | | | |
| status | | | | | | |
| survive | | | | | | |

🔑 Oxford 3000™ keywords

 **Outside the Reading** What do you know about urban planning?
Watch the video on the student website to find out more.

## Before You Read

Read these questions. Discuss your answers in a small group.

1. What is the biggest city you've ever visited? What did you like about it? Was there anything you didn't like? Why or why not?

2. How big is your city—in geographic size and in population? Would you say your city is small, medium-sized, large, or extremely large? Why?

3. Think about the cities near where you live. How near are other major cities? Are there any smaller suburban communities surrounding your city? What reasons or factors can you think of to explain the pattern of urban development in your area?

4. What other words do you know that start with the prefix *mega-*?

**MORE WORDS YOU'LL NEED**

**ecopolis:** a city considered in relationship to its environment (from the Greek "eco," meaning *house*, or more broadly *surroundings*, and "polis," meaning *city*)

**megalopolis:** an urban region, especially one consisting of several large cities and suburbs that are all connected to each other (from the Greek "mega," meaning *large*, and "polis," meaning *city*)

**REVIEW A SKILL** Previewing and Predicting (See p. 2)

Preview and predict the topic of Reading 1, using skills practiced in Unit 1. Look at the illustrations, scan for frequently used words and names of places, and skim the final paragraph.

## Read

This article from *Newsweek* magazine is about the rise of megacities.

# The New Megalopolis

*Our focus on cities is wrong. Growth and innovation come from new urban corridors.*

China isn't the world's most ferocious new economic competitor—the exploding east-coast corridor, from Beijing to Shanghai, is. India as a whole is not developing high-tech industries and attracting jobs, but the booming mega-region stretching from Bangalore to Hyderabad is. Across the world, in fact, nations don't spur growth so much as dynamic regions—modern versions of the original "megalopolis," a term coined by the geographer Jean Gottman to identify the sprawling Boston–New York–Washington economic power corridor in the United States.

The New Megas are the real economic organizing units of the world and the **major sources** of **global** wealth, attracting a large share of its talent and generating the most innovation. They take shape as powerful complexes of multiple cities and suburbs, often stretching across national borders—forming a vast expanse of trade, transport, **communications**, and talent. Yet, **despite** the fact that the rise of regions has been apparent for more than a decade, no one has collected systematic information on them—not the World Bank, not the IMF,[1] not the United Nations, not the **global** consulting firms.

That's why a team of geographers set about building a world map of the New Megas shaped by satellite images of the world at night, using light emissions to **define** the outlines of each region, and additional data in categories such as population and economic growth to chart their relative peak strengths and dynamism.[2]

The map makes it clear that the **global** economy takes shape around perhaps 20 great Megas scattered throughout the world. These regions are home to just 10 percent of total world population, 660 million people, but produce half of all economic activity, two-thirds of world-class scientific activity, and three quarters of **global** innovations. The great urbanologist Jane Jacobs was the first to describe why megalopolises grow. When people **migrate** to one place, they all become more productive. And the place itself becomes much more productive, because collective creativity grows exponentially.[3] Ideas flow more freely, are honed[4] more sharply, and can be put into practice more quickly.

There is, however, a tipping point.[5] The forces of price and congestion begin pushing people away from the center. But make no mistake, this has nothing to do with the "decentralization of work," as many have argued. The huge economic advantages of clustering still guide the process, which is why second cities emerge near big cities or in the corridors between them, not in the middle of nowhere.

The first region to achieve Mega **status** and still the biggest Mega in economic terms

 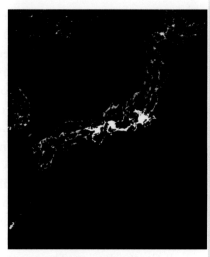

Satellite images of the Boston-to-Washington Mega-region in the United States (left) and the greater Tokyo Mega-region in Japan (right).

is the Boston-to-Washington corridor in the U.S. In 1961 it was home to about 32 million people; by 2025 its population is expected to rise to 58 million, or about 16 percent of all the U.S. population. The region generates $2.6 trillion in economic activity, making it the world's fourth largest economy, bigger than France or the United Kingdom. Next in line is Chi-Pitts, the great Midwestern Mega running from Chicago to Detroit, Cleveland, and Pittsburgh, with $2.1 trillion in economic activity. Three of the power centers of the U.S. economy even stretch beyond American borders: So-Cal runs from Los Angeles to San Diego across the Mexican border to Tijuana; Tor-Buff-Chester sprawls from Toronto, Ontario, to Rochester, New York; and Cascadia runs from Portland, Oregon, to Vancouver, British Colombia.

Aside from the island-bound financial center of Greater London, Europe's **major** economic engines do not **rely** on old borders to **define** themselves. The Euro-Lowlands cuts across four nations: the Netherlands, Belgium, Germany, and France. The Euro-Sunbelt stretches from Barcelona to Marseille, attracting people and firms with competitive costs and the Mediterranean lifestyle. Japan is less a country than a **network** of linked Mega-regions, anchored by Greater Tokyo: indeed, a close look at the light-emissions map shows that its three

---

[1] *IMF:* International Monetary Fund, a financial monitoring and regulating organization
[2] *dynamism:* the pattern or process of change, growth, and activity
[3] *exponentially:* extremely rapidly
[4] *honed:* sharpened
[5] *tipping point:* the moment at which a trend reaches its peak and starts to decline

**major** metro regions are blurring into a megalopolis of more than 100 million people.

100　While Mega-regions power advanced economies, they literally **define** the emerging nations. The world's largest concentration of megacities, one of ten mega-corridors in India, stretches from northwest India to Bangladesh 105 across the Indo-Gangetic plain and links a dozen **major** metropolitan areas. If you **removed** its Megas, China would be virtually meaningless as an economic category. What matters are the Shang-King (Shanghai to Nanjing) and Hong-Zen 110 (Hong Kong to Shenzhen) corridors and the area of Greater Beijing. Their combined regional

populations totaled more than 274 million people in 2010. These three Megas account for most of Chinese economic output, attract most 115 of its talent, and generate the great **majority** of its innovations.

Instead of technology helping to spread economic opportunity and lift many more boats, economic power is concentrating in a small 120 number of key regions. It's time for political and economic leadership to wake up to this new reality. It makes little sense to dwell on individual cities or countries anymore, when the real engines of **survival**, innovation, and growth 125 are the New Megas. ■

## Reading Comprehension

Mark each sentence as *T* (true) or *F* (false) according to the information in Reading 1. In your notebook, cite the location of the information by line number, and correct each false statement.

___ 1. Across the globe, nations create economic growth more than regions.

___ 2. Major international institutions such as the United Nations have been systematically collecting information about megacities.

___ 3. There are about 20 megacities scattered around the globe.

___ 4. The biggest mega-region is Chicago to Pittsburgh, in the United States.

___ 5. Mega-regions sometimes ignore borders and include more than one country.

___ 6. The three major Megas in China account for almost all of China's economic power.

___ 7. When older cities get too large, new cities emerge in the middle of nowhere.

___ 8. According to urbanologist Jane Jacobs, people become more productive and creative when they gather together in cities.

## READING SKILL　Identifying Main Ideas vs. Supporting Details

### LEARN

Writers offer specific details and examples to clarify and support their general ideas. When reading a text, it is helpful to identify both the main ideas and the supporting details and note these in a simple outline form.

### APPLY

**A.** Read these excerpts from Reading 1. Put a check (✓) next to the main ideas.

___ Nations don't spur growth as much as dynamic regions.

___ Today, its population has risen to 58 million.

___ Europe's major economic engines have even less respect for old borders.

___ The New Megas are the real economic organizing units of the world.

___ The global economy takes shape around perhaps 20 great Megas.

___ What matters are Shang-King (Shanghai to Nanjing) and Hong-Zen (Hong Kong to Shenzhen) corridors and the area of Greater Beijing.

___ The region generates $2.6 trillion in economic activity.

**B.** Reading 1 has nine paragraphs. What is the writer's main purpose in each? Write some notes (no sentences necessary) about the focus of each paragraph.

Paragraph 1: _explain idea of "mega"; give some examples of megas_
Paragraph 2: _____
Paragraph 3: _____
Paragraph 4: _____
Paragraph 5: _____
Paragraph 6: _____
Paragraph 7: _____
Paragraph 8: _____
Paragraph 9: _____

**C.** In your notebook, summarize the main idea of the entire article.

## Vocabulary Activities  STEP I: Word Level

A *network* is "an interconnected or interrelated chain, group, or system." There are various types of *networks*. The noun form is frequently combined with other nouns to make collocations, for example, a *computer network*.

The verb form of *network* means "to create social communication channels and mutual support systems." People *network* to advance their careers or to improve their social lives.

CORPUS

**A.** Match the type of network with its example. Use your dictionary to help you understand new words. Compare answers with a partner.

___ 1. CCTV (China Central) or BBC          a. computer network

___ 2. a company's intranet                 b. transportation network

___ 3. the Bill and Melinda Gates Foundation  c. television network

___ 4. the Paris metro                      d. communications network

___ 5. the human central nervous system     e. job network

___ 6. friends you meet through other friends  f. neural network

___ 7. satellite mobile phones              g. social network

___ 8. people you work with                 h. charity network

The word *migrate* means "move from one area to another." It is usually used to describe the seasonal movement of all types of migratory species.

*Salmon **migrate** to their birthplace every spring to lay their eggs.*

**Note**: *Migrate* is the root for two other words you probably know that describe movement of people from one country to another: *immigrate* (to move into another country) and *emigrate* (to move out of your own country). In addition, the related word *migrant* is used to describe workers who move from one area to another searching for work.

CORPUS

**B.** With a partner, think of three species (type of animal, bird, fish, or insect) that migrate, and then discuss what you know about them. Record your notes below. For each species, consider these things:

- departure point
- destination
- length of trip in time and distance
- how it finds its way
- the purpose of the migration

1. Species: _____

   Notes: _____

   _____

2. Species: _____

   Notes: _____

   _____

3. Species: _____

   Notes: _____

   _____

**C.** Complete the sentences about megacities using the target vocabulary in the box. Use each item one time. The synonyms in parentheses can help you.

| | | | |
|---|---|---|---|
| communications | global | network | survival |
| define | migrate | rely on | |

1. Megacities form a vast expanse of trade, transport, _____ ,
   (message systems)
   innovation, and talent.

2. The maps make it clear that the _____ economy takes shape
   (worldwide)
   around perhaps 20 great Megas.

3. Mega-regions compose a major part of advanced economies and actually

   _____ several emerging nations.
   (give complete form to)

4. Japan is less a country than a _____ of Mega-regions, anchored
   *(interconnected system)*
   by Greater Tokyo.

5. When many people _____ to one place, they all become more
   *(move)*
   productive.

6. The _____ of megacities will depend on their ability to adapt to
   *(continued existence)*
   the needs of their people and the environment.

7. Although many cities _____ imports for much of their food, fast-
   *(count on)*
   growing megacities are often incapable of organizing the food imports they
   need.

**D.** What are some sources for these items? Think globally and locally. Discuss your
answers in small groups. Choose the three most significant sources for each item.

1. information about traffic conditions
2. information for an essay on electricity usage
3. pollution
4. creativity

## Vocabulary Activities | STEP II: Sentence Level

**E.** *Status* has several meanings. Write your own definitions based on these example
sentences. Do not use your dictionary. Be prepared to compare and discuss your
definitions with a partner. You may check your dictionaries afterward.

1. The application asked for her age, her place of birth, her marital status, and a
   lot of other personal details.

   _____

   _____

2. Celebrities often have a higher status in society than regular people.

   _____

   _____

3. The foreman reported the status of the construction of the new administration
   building to the committee. He said it should be finished within six months.

   _____

   _____

The verb *rely* is actually a verb phrase because it always takes the preposition *on*. There are two typical structures for this verb phrase: "*Rely on* someone (or something) *for* something" is one:

> City planners **rely on** experts <u>for data</u> on population growth, traffic patterns, and ecological impact.

"*Rely on* someone (or something) *to do* something" is another:

> As cities become more crowded, residents **rely on** public transportation more and more <u>to get around town</u>.

CORPUS

| Word Form Chart | | | |
|---|---|---|---|
| **Noun** | **Verb** | **Adjective** | **Adverb** |
| reliance<br>relying (gerund)<br>reliability | rely (on) | reliable<br>unreliable | reliably |

**F.** **Complete these sentences using a form of *rely*. Be sure to use the verb phrase *rely on* where appropriate.**

1. He _____ his parents for money.

2. She always does what she promises to do. She is completely _____ .

3. He rarely asks for help. He believes that self-_____ is better than _____ on others.

4. His new car often breaks down. He can't depend on it; it is very _____ .

5. She _____ her friends to tell her the truth.

6. If you want to leave at 2:30, tell Mika to be here at 2:00. She is _____ late for everything!

7. This car was rated #1 in _____ and safety by automotive analysts.

**Now write four sentences of your own using four different forms of *rely*.**

1. *Unreliable technology doesn't survive for long in major global communications networks.*

2. _____

3. _____

4. _____

5. _____

## Before You Read

Read these questions. Be prepared to discuss your answers.

1. Where do the people in your city get all the food they need? What do they do with all their garbage?

2. What particular ecological challenges does your city have to deal with? What special policies or regulations are in place to help the city cope with these challenges? What do you think should be done to cope with them?

3. What impact do big cities have on the environment? Give examples to support your ideas.

## Read

This online article from *New Scientist* magazine discusses the ecological advantages of urban living.

# Ecopolis Now

*Forget the rural idyll. Urban living may be the best way to save the planet.*

A hundred years ago, the largest city in the world was London, with a population of 6.5 million. Today it is dwarfed by Tokyo. With barely a quarter the population of London a century ago,
5 the Tokyo metropolitan area has since mushroomed to 35 million, propelling it to first place in the **global** city league table. Tokyo's phenomenal growth is largely due to a single factor: **migration** from the countryside to the
10 city. It is just one of many to have overtaken London, which with a population of 7.5 million today doesn't even make the top 20.

This rural-to-urban **migration** can now be seen in scores of cities around the **globe**. And it has
15 brought us to a pivotal moment in human history. In 1900, most people lived in the countryside, with a little over 10 percent of the world's population living in cities. From next year, the UN Population Division predicts that for the first time
20 in history, more people will live in cities than in the country, and the biggest growth will be in "megacities," with populations over 10 million.

The meteoric growth of megacities—there are now more than 25 in total—has brought with it
25 huge environmental and social problems. Cities occupy just two percent of the land surface of the Earth but consume three-quarters of the resources that are used up each year, expelling the half-digested remains
30 in clouds of greenhouse gases, billions of tons of solid waste, and rivers of toxic sewage. Their inhabitants are making ruinous demands on soils and water supplies for food and on forests for timber and paper.

35 Returning the world's population to the countryside isn't an option. Dividing up the planet into plots of land on which we could all **survive** self-sufficiently would create its own natural disasters, not to mention being highly
40 unlikely to ever happen. If we are to protect what is left of nature, and meet the demand to improve the quality of living for the world's developing nations, a new form of city living is the only option. The size of a city creates
45 economies of scale for things such as energy generation, recycling, and public transport. It should even be possible for cities to partly feed themselves. Far from being parasites on

the world, cities could hold the key to sustainable living for the world's booming population—if they are built right.

Fortunately, governments, planners, architects, and engineers are beginning to wake up to this idea, and are dreaming up new ways to green the megacities. Their approaches **rely** on two main principles: recycle whatever possible and **remove** as many cars as possible. So as well as developing energy-efficient buildings, emphasis is being placed on increasing the use of public transport and redesigning how cities are organized to integrate work and living areas into a single neighborhood, rather than separating cities into residential, commercial, and industrial zones.

The big ideas are still being **defined**, but many cities already have showcase[1] eco-projects. For example, at the new home of Melbourne city council in Australia, hanging gardens and water fountains cool the air, wind turbines and solar cells generate up to 85 percent of the electricity used in the building, and rooftop rainwater collectors supply 70 percent of its water needs. In Berlin, Germany's new Reichstag parliament building cut its carbon dioxide emissions by 94 percent by **relying** on carbon-neutral vegetable oil as its energy **source**. In San Diego, California, garbage trucks run on methane **extracted** from the landfills they deliver to. In Austria, 1,500 free bicycles have been distributed across Vienna. Reykjavik in Iceland is among the pioneers of hydrogen-powered public transport, and Shanghai is subsidizing the installation of 100,000 rooftop solar panels. In Masdar, an emerging sustainable eco-city on the outskirts of Abu Dhabi in the United Arab Emirates, a modern version of the Arabian wind tower is used to cool urban plazas.

Planners and architects now agree that to improve the social and environmental condition of cities the top priority is to cut car use. They say zero-emission cars running on electricity or burning hydrogen are not enough. "Automobiles still require massive **networks** of streets, freeways, and parking structures to serve congested cities and far-flung suburbs," says Richard Register, founder of the nonprofit

In Masdar, this modern wind tower cools urban plazas.

campaigning organization EcoCity Builders in Oakland, California. What is needed is a wholesale rethink of how new cities are laid out—and how existing ones expand—to minimize the need for cars in the first place. One way of achieving this is to build cities with multiple centers where people live close to their work in high-rise blocks that are also near public transport hubs. In parts of the world this is already taking shape.

While planners look at how to cut back the energy consumption of big cities, at the other end of the scale are shanty towns—organically evolved and self-built by millions of people in the developing world without a planner in sight. These shanties meet many of the ideals of eco-city designers. They are high-density but low-rise; their lanes and alleys are largely pedestrianized; and many of their inhabitants recycle waste materials from the wider city. From a purely ecological **perspective**, shanties and their inhabitants are a good example of the new, green urban metabolism.[2] **Despite**

---

[1] *showcase:* publicized in a positive way
[2] *metabolism:* way of using energy

their sanitary and security failings, they often have a social vibrancy and sound ecological **status** that
120 gets lost in most planned urban environments.

So perhaps something can be taken from the chaos and decentralized spontaneity embodied in shanties, and combined with the planned infrastructure of a designed eco-city. Cities built
125 without extensive high rises can still be dense enough to make life without a car profitable, and they can retain the economies of scale needed for the new metabolism built around efficient recycling of everything from sewage
130 to sandwich wrappers. At the same time, they need to remain flexible enough for people to adapt them to the way they want to live.

## Reading Comprehension

Mark each sentence as *T* (true) or *F* (false) according to the information in Reading 2, and locate the answer by line number. Correct each false statement in your notebook.

___ 1. Urban migration is a global trend.

___ 2. Megacities have brought about few ecological or social problems.

___ 3. Returning to the countryside is a good alternative for modern city dwellers if megacities create significant problems.

___ 4. Governments and planners know that megacities need to become more ecology-minded.

___ 5. The top priority of urban planners is to decrease car use.

___ 6. Planners are trying to minimize the need for cars by rethinking the way cities are laid out.

___ 7. From a purely ecological perspective, unplanned shanty towns are possible models for the future.

___ 8. Megacities are not expected to grow much more than they already have.

## READING SKILL    Identifying Main Ideas vs. Supporting Details

### LEARN

Reread the article on pages 25–27. As you read each paragraph, think about the writer's main purpose. Then create an outline below by identifying the main ideas and supporting details.

Paragraph 1, Main Idea: *Tokyo is now the biggest city in the world.*

    Supporting detail: *It has 35 million people.*

    Supporting detail: *It's much bigger than London, a former #1.*

Paragraph 2, Main Idea: _____

    Supporting detail: _____

    Supporting detail: _____

Paragraph 3, Main Idea: _____

    Supporting detail: _____

    Supporting detail: _____

Paragraph 4, Main Idea: _____

    Supporting detail: _____

    Supporting detail: _____

Paragraph 5, Main Idea: _____

    Supporting detail: _____

    Supporting detail: _____

Paragraph 6, Main Idea: _____

    Supporting detail: _____

    Supporting detail: _____

Paragraph 7, Main Idea: _____

    Supporting detail: _____

    Supporting detail: _____

Paragraph 8, Main Idea: _____

    Supporting detail: _____

    Supporting detail: _____

Paragraph 9, Main Idea: _____

    Supporting detail: _____

    Supporting detail: _____

**Now, in your notebook, summarize the main idea of the entire article:**

## Vocabulary Activities    STEP I: Word Level

**A.**   With a partner, complete the word form chart. Use your dictionary to help you.
Then complete the sentences that follow using the correct form of *communicate*.

| Word Form Chart for *Communicate* | | |
| --- | --- | --- |
| **Noun** | **Verb** | **Adjective** |
| 1. (a person): _____ <br> 2. (thing, singular): _____ <br> 3. (thing, plural): _____ | communicate | 1. _____ <br> 2. communicable |

1. He talked openly and honestly about the problem. He was very

    _____ .

2. She speaks clearly and enthusiastically. She's an effective _____ .

3. Regular _____ is an important part of any business or social
relationship.

4. Computers and cell phones have completely changed modern

    _____ .

5. The committee members disagree, but they must _____ with
each other in order to reach a compromise and settle the issue.

6. Some diseases are passed genetically from parent to child. Others are
_____—they pass from one person to another through contact.

**B.** Complete these sentences from another *New Scientist* article, "Urban Appetite," using the target vocabulary in the box. Use each item once.

| | | | |
|---|---|---|---|
| communications | extracting | network | status |
| defined | globe | rely | survived |
| despite | major | sources | |

1. The megacity is _____ as a city with a population of more than
   *(specifically described)*
   ten million.

2. Sometime around 1940, New York City was the first to reach megacity
   _____ .
   *(rank or standing)*

3. Extensive transport networks, the boom in cheap _____ , and
   *(technological message systems)*
   cultural changes in work and living have contributed to the rise of megacities.

4. Feeding a city is not easy. Unable or unwilling to _____
   *(depend)*
   on distant _____ for food, many cities are substantially
   *(supply origins)*
   feeding themselves.

5. In the early 1990s, the Bosnian capital of Sarajevo _____ a siege
   *(stayed alive)*
   by cultivating its wasteland.

6. Water managers believe that governments should make city sewage safe for
   irrigation and fertilization by _____ disease-causing pathogens
   *(taking out)*
   while leaving the nutrients.

7. "Eco-cities must be farming cities," says Jac Smit, president of UAN, the Urban
   Agriculture _____ run by the United Nations Development Program.
   *(interconnected group)*

8. _____ the _____ social and ecological challenges
   *(even though there are)*   *(very big)*
   they present, megacities around the _____ can and must be
   *(earth)*
   jointly adapted to both people and planet.

**C.** Give three examples of these things. Discuss your answers with a partner. Why do you think your examples are *major*?

1. a major artist: *Leonardo da Vinci* _____
   _____

2. a major river: _____

   _____

3. a major catastrophe: _____

   _____

4. a major scientific achievement: _____

   _____

5. a major improvement in human life: _____

   _____

The word *major* also has an academic meaning. As a noun, it means "a field of study chosen as an academic specialty." It can also describe a student specializing in such studies.

> *He finally decided on urban planning as a **major.***

> *He is an architecture **major.***

As a verb, *major* means "to pursue academic studies in a particular subject."

> *She is **majoring** in mathematics.*

Some students major in two subjects. This is called *double majoring* and students are called *double majors*.

> *He is double **majoring** in political science and geography.*

CORPUS

**D.** Imagine your friends ask you for advice about what major they should choose. For each profession, which major(s) would you recommend? Discuss your reasons in a small group.

1. humanitarian aid worker
2. factory pollution inspector
3. tax collector
4. executive assistant
5. magazine editor
6. television producer

## Vocabulary Activities  STEP II: Sentence Level

*Despite* is a preposition used to show contrasts or opposites of action, thought, or expectation.

> ***Despite** their sanitary and security failings, shanty towns often have social vibrancy and sound ecological status.*

You can also use the phrase *the fact that* to connect clauses.

> ***Despite** <u>the fact that</u> the rise of regions has been apparent for more than a decade, no one has collected systematic information on them.*

**Note:** *In spite of* has the exact same meaning as *despite* and can be used in the same grammatical structures.

> ***In spite of** their sanitary and security failings, shanty towns often have social vibrancy and sound ecological status.*

> ***In spite of** <u>the fact that</u> the rise of regions has been apparent for more than a decade, no one has collected systematic information on them.*

CORPUS

**E.** Write four sentences featuring information you have learned about cities. Use the words in parentheses in your sentences.

1. (despite)

_____

_____

2. (in spite of)

_____

_____

3. (despite the fact that)

_____

_____

4. (in spite of the fact that)

_____

_____

**F.** Read the definitions of *perspective*. Decide which meaning applies to each sample sentence. Then rewrite the sample sentences without using the target word.

> a. creating the appearance of objects in depth on a flat surface
> b. the ability to view things in their true relation or relative importance
> c. the viewpoint or position of a particular person or group

___ 1. It was difficult for the mayor to maintain a realistic perspective of the traffic problem after she was in a car accident.

_____

_____

___ 2. The students are using a new computer program that depicts city streets and buildings in perspective.

_____

_____

___ 3. From the environmental group's perspective, any law allowing cars into the city center should be opposed as unsafe and unhealthy for citizens.

_____

_____

**G.** Self-Assessment Review: Go back to page 17 and reassess your knowledge of the target vocabulary. How has your understanding of the words changed? What words do you feel most comfortable with now?

## Writing and Discussion Topics

**Write about or discuss the following topics.**

1. Think about the career of urban planning. What kinds of training, experience, and knowledge do you think an urban planner should possess today? What should someone interested in urban planning major in? What difficulties will urban planners of the future face?

2. Should the environmental issues raised by megacities be dealt with on a city level, country level, regional level, or global level?

3. What is (or will be) your major? How did you (will you) decide what subject to major in? Do you think it is better to major in something you enjoy or something that will help you get a good job?

# UNIT 3

# In the Public Eye

## In this unit, you will

> read about some public art exhibits and the issues they raise for artists and communities.
> review identifying main ideas vs. supporting details
> increase your understanding of the target academic words for this unit.

**READING SKILL** Skimming and Making Predictions

## Self-Assessment
Think about how well you know each target word, and check (✓) the appropriate column. I have...

| TARGET WORDS | never seen the word before | seen the word but am not sure what it means | seen the word and understand what it means | used the word, but am not sure if correctly | used the word confidently in *either* speaking *or* writing | used the word confidently in *both* speaking *and* writing |
|---|---|---|---|---|---|---|
| **AWL** | | | | | | |
| 🔑 comment | | | | | | |
| 🔑 criteria | | | | | | |
| 🔑 ethnic | | | | | | |
| 🔑 fund | | | | | | |
| 🔑 goal | | | | | | |
| guideline | | | | | | |
| inspect | | | | | | |
| 🔑 interpret | | | | | | |
| legislate | | | | | | |
| mutual | | | | | | |
| ongoing | | | | | | |
| 🔑 policy | | | | | | |
| rational | | | | | | |
| 🔑 topic | | | | | | |

🔑 Oxford 3000™ keywords

**Outside the Reading** What do you know about art and design? Watch the video on the student website to find out more.

## Before You Read

Read these questions. Discuss your answers in a small group.

1. Have you been to an art gallery or art museum? What did you like or not like about that experience?

2. What is different about the experience of seeing art outside, compared with going to an art gallery or museum?

3. How would you define "public art"? What types of things would this include? What, do you think, is its purpose?

## READING SKILL | Skimming and Making Predictions

### LEARN

Pre-reading skills can help you read more quickly and understand important ideas more completely. One important pre-reading skill is skimming for main ideas and making predictions. "Skimming" means reading quickly, looking for important ideas, but not focusing on every word you see, and not reading entire sentences.

### APPLY

Follow these steps to preview and make predictions about "Art Attack" on page 36.

First, read the title and the subtitle and look at the photograph. Write a guess about the topic of the reading.

*I think this article will be about* _____ .

Second, read the first paragraph and the last paragraph. Do you think your first guess was correct? If not, write a new guess, or add more specific information to your first guess.

*I think this article will be about* _____ .

Next, look at the headings (the words in capital letters) that begin each section of the article. *Don't read the paragraphs—only the headings.* For each heading, think of one or two questions that you think the section might answer. Try to ask about the most important ideas you think each section might discuss.

Heading 1: Public Art versus Museum Art

Question 1a: *How do public artworks differ from museum artworks?* ____ ?

Question 1b: _____ ?

Heading 2: _____

Question 2a: _____ ?

Question 2b: _____ ?

Heading 3: _____

  Question 3a: _____ ?

  Question 3b: _____ ?

Finally, make a guess about the main idea of the article.

Main idea: _____

As you read the article, think about the questions you thought of. How well did you anticipate the information in each section?

## 🔊 Read

The introduction and following article are about public art.

# Public Art Controversies

Cities invest in public art to attract tourists and add interest to their streets, but public art often causes controversy.[1] For example, consider Seoul, South Korea, which
5 instituted a **policy** that builders of large projects had to pay for a public art piece. Many residents were not pleased with some of the resulting art. Although the **guidelines** were recently changed, the unpopular sculptures remain, and there is an
10 **ongoing** debate about what to do with them.

Even the extremely popular Cow Parade has been a **topic** of controversy in a few areas. Since 1999, fiberglass[2] cows have been installed temporarily in over 50 cities worldwide. The cows
15 are decorated in different ways—painted with bright colors, dressed in **ethnic** clothing, or covered with mirrors or flowers by local artists— and then auctioned off to raise money for charity. But some residents have questioned whether the
20 cows are really art; they think the animals look cheap or are not in good taste, and some have objected to the decoration of particular cows.

The following article was written in response to a controversy about a public sculpture in
25 Phoenix, Arizona. Before the sculpture went up, many citizens felt that the city shouldn't spend

"Her Secret Is Patience," Phoenix, Arizona, USA

$2.4 million on the project, and for a while it looked like the city might back out.

Since it was completed, the work, called "Her
30 Secret Is Patience," has earned several awards and has been well received by the local residents. It's a large transparent[3] structure that appears to float above the city. The artist, Janet Echelman, says it "makes visible to the human eye the patterns of
35 desert winds." During the day, the piece casts patterned shadows on the ground. At night, its bright colors slowly change through the seasons. Echelman has a number of public art pieces in many cities, including Richmond, British Columbia; Porto,
40 Portugal; Madrid, Spain; and Rotterdam, Netherlands.

---

[1] *controversy:* disagreement
[2] *fiberglass:* a plastic material that includes glass fibers
[3] *transparent:* clear; see-through

# Art Attack

*Public installations have been angering residents ever since the Parthenon went up in Greece.*

Ah, public art. The very words suggest committee battles and last-minute vetoes. But if you think people are usually arguing over how these artworks actually look or what they 45 represent, think again. In most cases what upsets people is location, durability,[4] safety, effect on property values, traffic patterns, how to **fund** the project, and other logistical issues, says Bob Lynch, president and CEO 50 of a nonprofit organization that oversees public arts programs.

## PUBLIC ART VERSUS MUSEUM ART

In 1999, San Diego public arts administrators rejected a proposal for a sculpture built from boat scraps[5] because residents thought it 55 would be too weird for the proposed location downtown. So the artist, Nancy Rubins, took her work to a museum a few miles away, and it quickly became a hit. "It's been used extensively in articles and travel magazines. 60 It has become a favorite image of the area," says Denise Montgomery, spokeswoman for the Museum of Contemporary Art in nearby La Jolla. The arrangement had **mutual** benefits for the public and the museum. But Robert 65 Pincus, art critic for the *San Diego Union-Tribune,* is quick to point out why: "Now people don't complain about it. Part of the reason they don't is that it's on museum grounds. Museums can do what they want. But 70 if it was out in public, they'd be outraged."

## CAUSES OF CONTROVERSY

It could be that in modern times, artists are finding it harder to make a statement. Many artists have used art to try to surprise or shock people. But Kim Babon, a sociologist of art at 75 Wake Forest University who studied hundreds of people's reactions to sculptures, found that context, not content, is what people care about the most. "People were concerned with the way art fits in the urban environment," **comments** 80 Babon. What it comes down to is the flow of daily life: does a sculpture in a plaza break your routine by forcing you to take a different route to work? Does it break a city's routine by reducing use of a parking lot or park? And, just 85 as important, does it break your visual habits or associations with a certain space? Babon says that people learn to care about a place because it has a particular meaning or because they use the place for a particular purpose. If 90 an artwork seems to conflict with the meaning of the place or if it interferes with the way they use it, they are not happy.

## LESSONS WE'VE LEARNED

If history reveals anything, it's that the art often outlives the controversy it creates. A senator 95 once complained about some modern buildings making his city look cheap, and the architect was jailed. Lynch says all kinds of people wrote negative **comments** about how the city was wasting money on extremely ugly, distasteful 100 objects. This senator lived in Athens almost 2,500 years ago, and was complaining about buildings such as the Parthenon! Now just try imagining Athens without the Parthenon and the other buildings on the Acropolis.

**The Parthenon, Athens, Greece**

105 The same goes for the Eiffel Tower and Pablo Picasso's 1967 Chicago sculpture. Interestingly, Picasso's was privately **funded**, meaning that the city's money was not involved, but the work still caused controversy. Both 110 works occupy prime spots on public land and

---

[4] *durability:* ability to last or stay in good condition
[5] *scraps:* small pieces

were widely disliked at the time they were built. Nowadays, however, both are easily recognized symbols of the cities where they are located and don't seem the least bit controversial. Scandal may have propelled them to fame, but over time something else kicked in: people got used to them and eventually grew to love them.

According to some public arts administrators, one way to reduce controversy is to involve the public in the decision process, so the space is used in the way that appeals to the most people. Another trend is integrating public art into the surrounding space. Artists are expected to consider the use and appearance of the area in their designs. Gone are the days of "plop art," when works were erected by a select group of experts without considering public opinion. Increasingly, public art is designed by architects with the **goal** of blending harmoniously with buildings or planned spaces. Of course, if art is forced to meet rigid **criteria**, the risk is that it could become merely decorative. And the worst artistic offense of all, says Pincus, is blandness. Janet Echelman, a well-known public artist, says controversy is a good thing. "It's good for art to make us think, to give us a shared experience that creates a dialogue, makes us talk to each other, including strangers." So whether they call it unsightly or elegantly beautiful, at least there'll be something to whisper about. The stranger the better? ■

## Reading Comprehension

Circle the best answer to the questions. Skim the article to help you find the answers.

1. What is the public-art debate in Seoul about?

   a. How to fund art projects

   b. The location of public art projects

   c. What to do with unpopular public art

   d. How much to spend on public art

2. What was the controversy about "Her Secret Is Patience"?

   a. The size of the project

   b. The price of the project

   c. The location of the project

   d. The appearance of the project

3. What did Nancy Rubins do when her public art sculpture was rejected?

   a. She moved it to a museum.

   b. She moved it to a different country.

   c. She destroyed it.

   d. She changed it.

4. What most often upsets people about public art?

   a. It's shocking.

   b. It's unattractive.

   c. It causes problems with traffic.

   d. It changes a place they care about.

5. How are cities making public art less controversial?

    a. They are asking residents for their opinions about future projects.

    b. They are assigning a panel of experts to choose the work.

    c. They are trying to put up bland art.

    d. They are telling residents, "The stranger the better."

**REVIEW A SKILL** **Identifying Main Ideas vs. Supporting Details** (See p. 20)

Review Reading 1. What is the main idea of each paragraph? Which details support each main idea? Write your answers in your notebook.

## Vocabulary Activities STEP I: Word Level

**A.** Match each word on the left with its meaning (or meanings) on the right. For the words with more than one meaning, circle the meaning that is used in Reading 1. Compare your answers with a partner.

| | |
|---|---|
| ___ 1. ongoing | a. rules |
| ___ 2. fund | b. to mention (*v*), statement (*n*) |
| ___ 3. ethnic | c. to finance (*v*), money (*n*) |
| ___ 4. goal | d. objective |
| ___ 5. guidelines | e. in progress, incomplete |
| ___ 6. topic | f. subject |
| ___ 7. mutual | g. national, racial |
| ___ 8. comment | h. shared |

**B.** Read these sentences about city public art programs. For each sentence, cross out the one word or phrase in parentheses with a different meaning from the other three choices. Compare your answers with a partner.

1. Many cities have (*continuing / ongoing / momentary / long-term*) public art programs that produce new works on a regular basis.

2. Some cities have a (*rule / policy / law / limit*) requiring that a certain percentage of the budget be used to fund public art.

3. In order to receive government support, proposals must follow certain (*guidelines / styles / rules / specifications*) for public art.

4. Local governments use many different (*factors / resources / considerations / criteria*) when deciding what public art projects to fund.

5. The (*problem / goal / aim / purpose*) of local government is to (*fund / enable / support / repair*) new public art projects that provide opportunities for community involvement.

6. Public art projects are successful because local government and members of the community feel a (*common / ongoing / mutual / two-way*) responsibility to keep them clean and attractive, so the two groups cooperate in maintaining them.

7. Some public art (*comments on / refers to / speaks to / covers up*) problems in the local area, while other exhibits have no political message.

8. Some public art promotes understanding of and respect for diversity. For example, an artwork can express (*cultural / ethnic / national / selfish*) pride.

**C.** Read this passage about the different kinds of public art and their significance to local communities. Fill in the blanks using the target vocabulary in the box. The synonyms in parentheses can help you.

| | | | |
|---|---|---|---|
| commented | funded | mutual | topic |
| criteria | goals | ongoing | |
| ethnic | guidelines | policy | |

People have different viewpoints when they discuss the _____ of
(1. *aims*)
public art. However, the most important _____ for deciding whether
(2. *factors*)
something is public art are its availability and accessibility to the community.

Sometimes, city government requests a public art project. Often, cities have a
"percent for art" _____ with _____ showing how to use
(3. *rule*)          (4. *recommendations*)
a certain percentage of the budget for art. Some public art projects are initiated by
artists. The artist decides on a _____ for a project and then convinces
(5. *subject*)
the community and a sponsor that it is a worthwhile project.

In other cases, public art projects are started by communities that want to
improve the appearance of their neighborhoods, for example by using
_____ art to celebrate the culture of local residents.
(6. *cultural*)

Public art has many different forms and functions, both when it is created and
in its _____ existence. A mural is a good example. Some cities have
(7. *continuing*)
_____ more murals than any other kind of public art project. Murals
(8. *given money for*)
are painted in many places, including on walls, bus shelters, and even trash cans.

No matter where it is located, however, a mural has far-reaching effects. Glenna
B. Avilaan, an arts program director, has _____ that murals are about
(9. *said*)
the _____ respect and affection between people and their cities, with
(10. *shared*)
artists from the community taking responsibility for their visual and physical
environment, and, in the process, changing neighborhoods, decreasing vandalism,
and creating new artists in the community.

*Criteria* is the plural form of *criterion*. The plural form is far more commonly used than the singular form.

*Criteria* means "the standards that you use when you make a decision or form an opinion." For example, to decide what kind of car to buy, the usual criteria are price, size, gas mileage, safety, and whether it has extra things you might want, like a satellite radio.

CORPUS

**D.** Work in a small group to decide the three most important criteria for deciding these things.

1. the kind of apartment or house you want to live in

   _____    _____    _____

2. the kind of person you would like to be friends with

   _____    _____    _____

3. the best kind of animal for a pet

   _____    _____    _____

4. the best modern athlete

   _____    _____    _____

5. the most important invention of all time

   _____    _____    _____

## Vocabulary Activities  STEP II: Sentence Level

**E.** Read these sentences about art in Dubai. Rephrase them in your notebook using the target vocabulary in parentheses.

1. The Dubai International Financial Center pays for Art Dubai, an art festival whose main purpose is to provide cultural programming and support for the arts in the Middle East. (*fund, goal*)

   *The Dubai International Financial Center funds Art Dubai, an art festival whose main goal is to provide cultural programming and support for the arts in the Middle East.*

2. Artists from many different cultural backgrounds participate in the festival; one gallery manager said she likes to feature artists of diverse backgrounds and works of different media. (*ethnic, comment*)

3. The festival's Global Arts Forum explores issues that are of interest to the Middle East, North Africa, South Asia, and the rest of the world. (*topic, mutual*)

4. The festival takes place in the spring, but planning and preparation continue throughout the year. (*ongoing*)

To *fund* means "to give money for a project or a business." A *fund* is an account that exists to give money to a certain person or purpose. *Funds* (plural only) is a synonym for money. *Funding* is money that a project or organization receives to help with its work.

> City governments often **fund** public art projects.
>
> Many cities have a special **fund** for public art projects.
>
> Many organizations that produce public art have limited **funds.**
>
> These organizations rely on **funding** from charitable organizations and local government.

CORPUS

**F.** In your notebook, restate these sentences so that they include a form of *fund*. Share your sentences in a small group. How many different ways were you able to use *fund* in each case?

1. A new public art display in Shanghai is sponsored by the Shanghai Cultural Development Foundation and Shanghai Urban Sculpture Committee Office. The exhibit includes more than 200 sculptures by 70 artists from around the world.

2. Even people who don't have any money for artistic entertainment can see the display because it is free.

3. Liu Jianhua, a sculpture professor at Shanghai University, is pleased to see that the government is now providing financial support for public art.

4. In the past, Liu commented that there have not been many sculpture displays in town due to insufficient space and money.

5. If this show is successful, perhaps the government will create an account to generate money for public art.

6. Government contributions would certainly help the city to improve the quality of its public art.

**G.** Read the explanations and descriptions of public art in Activities B and C. Imagine that you are a journalist who is going to interview your local city government about its policy for funding public art, the history of public art in your city, and current public art displays. Prepare interview questions using the cues provided. Then role-play the interview with a partner.

1. which/criteria

   *Which criteria do you use to evaluate proposals for public art?*

2. what/fund

3. do/ethnic

4. what/topic

5. what/guidelines

6. who/policy

7. what/goal

8. when/ongoing

## Before You Read

**Read these questions. Discuss your answers in a small group.**

1. Have you ever seen art that you did not think should be considered art? Why did you think so?

2. Who should make decisions about what is art? What criteria should they use?

3. Is it possible for art to be bad, or must anything that is considered art also be considered good art?

## READING SKILL   Skimming and Making Predictions

### APPLY

Follow these steps to preview and make predictions about Reading 2.

First, read the title and look at the picture. Write a guess about the topic of the reading.

*I think this article will be about* _____ .

Second, read the first paragraph and the last paragraph. Do you think your first guess was correct? If not, write a new guess, or add more specific information to your first guess.

*I think this article will be about* _____ .

Next, look at the first sentence of each paragraph. *Don't read the whole paragraph—only the first sentence.* For each sentence, think of one or two questions that you think the paragraph might answer and write them in your notebook. Try to ask about the most important ideas you think each paragraph might discuss.

*Paragraph 1: Who does not like the street art?*

Finally, make a guess about the main idea of the article.

Main idea: _____

As you read the article, think about the questions you thought of. How well did you anticipate the information in each paragraph?

# One Person's Vandalism Is Another One's Art

BY LENORE COSTELLO

Some call it a plague and an eyesore; others consider it an expression of their basic rights. Some of it has deep political meaning, while some is a word or two written
5 quickly in permanent marker. And it can be found all over cities around the world: on rooftops, bridges, the walls of abandoned buildings. Graffiti and street art have been highly controversial forms of expression for
10 decades, hated by art snobs and building caretakers alike. The people who complain about it the most, however, are the city officials who clash with artists and taggers over their creations. Interestingly, this battle has done
15 nothing to lessen street art's popularity. And now, some experts say, that popularity could do what city officials couldn't: threaten the very essence of this short-lived art form.

A graffiti artist

What exactly are street art and graffiti? For
20 the graffiti artists, the **goal** is to "tag," or write their name, on the most places. Extra respect goes to those who get their tag on hard-to-reach spots, like billboards and the tops of high buildings. "If there are two graffiti artists, they
25 will compete for fame. They might never meet, but they compete because they see each others' names so much," said graffiti artist BG 183 of Tats Cru, a group of professional muralists.

Street art, on the other hand, usually has a
30 political or social message and aims to encourage the viewer to think and **interpret** ideas. Although street art is usually illegal like graffiti, many consider it an alternative art form, valuable to the community at large.

35 "Street art will only hit certain areas—rich areas—next to museums or galleries where people with money will see and notice it. They don't go to tunnels or the side of a highway. They won't risk getting caught," said BG 183.

40 "Graffiti is used in the broader sense, and street art is sometimes classified as a subset of graffiti," said Dave Combs, co-creator of the street art *Peel Magazine*. But, he continued, while some graffiti artists are partly motivated
45 by committing destruction or vandalism, "for the most part, people who do street art do it to create something new and meaningful and beautiful for the person viewing it."

City councils, though, often do not share
50 that view or distinguish much between street art and graffiti. They see both as a public annoyance that damages the quality of life in neighborhoods and communities, and they worry that any form of illegal street art makes
55 vandalism seem acceptable and lowers property values. To fight it, cities paint over walls, arrest or ticket graffiti artists, and even pass **legislation** forbidding anyone less than 21 years old to carry spray paint. However, some cities

have a different approach. São Paolo, Melbourne, and Taipei have established areas where graffiti is legal, hoping to allow artistic expression while discouraging vandalism.

## INTO THE MAINSTREAM

While efforts to combat street art continue, its acceptance seems to be growing in the cultural world, which may not be good for "real" street art. As its acceptance has grown, street art has started showing up everywhere. There are books about the **topic**, it is the main focus of magazines, and blogs display daily photos of street art from more and more cities around the world. A city's well-known street art appears in guides for tourists. Visitors to Berlin can even take a class on street art as they study local examples.

Some artists have stopped limiting themselves to using the streets as a canvas and begun using actual canvases, which then sell in galleries for high prices. Street art has been featured in world-renowned museums and gallery shows. Banksy, the world's most famous street artist, has sold individual pieces for tens of thousands of pounds, and celebrities are buying works by street artists from Brazil and Japan. Thousands of visitors came to **inspect** the work in a 2011 street art museum exhibit in Los Angeles while neighbors complained that because of the exhibit, more graffiti was appearing on nearby walls. Major companies pay graffiti artists to do advertisements for them. They spray-paint cars, soft drinks and shoes on walls and plaster up posters with a street-art aesthetic.[1]

## ARTISTS VS. STREET ART

As street art moves more into the mainstream, some critics fear it will lose its essential edginess. "The Splasher," an unidentified person or group of people, splashed paint on a number of works by famous street artists from late 2006 to 2007. Believing that street art had become too commercial and mainstream, the Splasher felt the only way to counter it was through destruction.

But many feel that the popularity of street art is going to lead to its disappearance without any destruction necessary. The argument is that street art is a fad, and that people spending large sums for it today are going to regret it in the future when they realize the work has no lasting value. After all, street art is not supposed to be permanent—it is meant to be washed away by the elements, painted over, or built on top of. It is created quickly and often deals with current and local issues. All of these aspects, say critics, mean that the art loses its aesthetic value when taken off the streets, and that it is **rational** to assume that such art will lose its economic value when it goes out of style. ■

---

[1] *aesthetic:* related to beauty and visual style

# Reading Comprehension

Circle the best answer to the questions. Skim the article to help you find the answers.

1. What is the goal of graffiti artists?
   a. To send a political message
   b. To have people think about ideas
   c. To write their names in the most places
   d. To create something beautiful

2. According to BG 183, where do people create street art?
   a. Tunnels
   b. Places rich people will see it
   c. Museums
   d. Sides of highways

3. Why don't city councils like street art?

    a. It's too commercial.

    b. It's a fad.

    c. It lowers property values.

    d. It's too expensive.

4. Why did "The Splasher" destroy street art?

    a. The Splasher thought it was too mainstream.

    b. The Splasher thought it didn't have lasting value.

    c. The Splasher thought it was vandalism.

    d. The Splasher thought it damaged the quality of life.

5. What do some critics say about buying street art?

    a. It's a good investment.

    b. It's going to be washed away by the elements.

    c. It's too mainstream.

    d. It's going to lose its value when it goes out of style.

## Vocabulary Activities   STEP I: Word Level

| Word Form Chart | | | |
|---|---|---|---|
| **Noun** | **Verb** | **Adjective** | **Adverb** |
| inspector<br>inspection | inspect | _____ | _____ |
| _____ | _____ | mutual | mutually |
| rationalization | rationalize | rational<br>irrational | rationally |
| legislator<br>legislation<br>legislature | legislate | legislative | _____ |
| ethnicity | _____ | ethnic | ethnically |

**A.** Fill in the blanks with a target word from the chart in the correct form. Use your dictionary to help understand new words. Compare answers with a partner.

1. There has been a big increase in the amount of graffiti on public buildings lately. In fact, the state _legislature_ is considering a law making it a crime to paint on buildings.

2. However, local artists are concerned this law will affect public art, which they argue is _____ beneficial. The city gets an increase in tourism, and artists get some attention that can lead to more commissions.

3. The artists _____ public art displays by arguing that any exposure to art is a positive thing.

4. The artists' group recognizes that some forms of public art, especially graffiti-style artwork, don't appeal to everyone. Many people see graffiti art as uncontrolled, _____ , and silly.

5. However, the artists point to several recently successful pieces of public art, particularly a critically acclaimed African mural. The bold colors and wild patterns in the mural were _____ inspired. The artist's family emigrated here from Kenya and she uses a lot of cultural images in her work.

6. At first, the mural looked like a thick jungle of vines and plants. Upon closer _____ , however, you could see human and animal forms moving through the greenery.

7. The artists also argued that the state already has substantial control over public art, since a state engineer must _____ every piece of art before it is approved for display.

**B.** Read these sentences about organizing a public art exhibit. Then, go back and restate each of them in your notebook using the words in parentheses as indicated. Do not change the meanings of the sentences. Discuss your sentences in a small group.

1. Like other kinds of art, public art projects come in many forms, and the resultant aim can be permanent or temporary art. (*goal, ongoing*)

2. Public art can have a sole author with a unique voice, or many participants with multiple viewpoints. (*interpret* or *interpretation*)

3. A good public art project requires the organizers to establish rules that include clearly defined guidelines for reviewing proposals and selecting the project. (*policy, criteria*)

4. A logical evaluation process should be used even if money is being used to create a community-based art project, rather than one done by a paid artist. (*rational, fund* or *funds*)

*Rational* means "reasonable, sensible, or logical." Likewise, *rationally* means "sensibly or logically." A *rationale* is a reason to do something. These are usually used in positive or unemotional contexts.

> *Decisions about how to use public money must be made **rationally,** with careful consideration given to many criteria.*

The verb to *rationalize* means "to find reasons to explain why you have done something." It is used in situations where there probably is not a good reason, but the person is trying to pretend there is.

> *Although some art experts find animal displays unimpressive, they **rationalize** them by arguing that they increase interest in "real" art.*

CORPUS

**C.** Read this essay discussing the author's frustration with the public art selection process. In your notebook, summarize the reasons the author gives for his opinion. Use different forms of *rational* in your summary. Discuss your summary in a small group. How many forms of *rational* was your group able to use?

One reason that public art is so terrible is that the entire process is controlled by idiotic bureaucrats and political appointees, many of whom are completely ignorant about art. Because public art offices are part of local government, poor artistic works are often chosen by someone with a low position who justifies his or her choice by saying it was politically necessary.

The selection of projects to receive state funding is done by a committee whose members are rarely selected using sensible criteria. Many members of the committee do not have an ongoing commitment to public art and don't have the education needed to logically consider the merits of different works. Some members do not see the value of "art for art's sake." They give an explanation of their choices based on whether they think the art will help the local economy.

Artists whose pieces are not chosen are often disappointed because they don't understand the reason their work was rejected.

**D.** Look at these arguments for and against animal art displays, such as the Cow Parades (discussed on page 35), that have been popular in recent years. Restate each idea in your notebook, using the word in parentheses. Then write a paragraph that expresses your own opinion. Try to use as many target words as possible in your work. Be prepared to debate this issue in class.

| For | Against |
|---|---|
| Children, parents, and grandparents can spend quality time at these exhibits, because they can discuss a shared experience. (*mutual*) | Animal parades do not have any of the qualities that are generally used to decide if something should be considered art. (*criteria*) |
| Displays like Cow Parade have successfully achieved their objective of bringing in shoppers to struggling businesses. (*goal*) | This phenomenon is continuous, with no end in sight, and as more locations follow the trend, the individual identities of the cities are lost. (*ongoing*) |
| Many young artists see animal art displays as a chance to bring their own ideas and understanding of a theme to a wider audience. (*interpretation, topic*) | Laws that fund public art only allow for a certain amount of money each year, so anything spent on a Cow Parade is taken away from legitimate art. (*legislation*) |

**E.** Self-Assessment Review: Go back to page 33 and reassess your knowledge of the target vocabulary. How has your understanding of the words changed? What words do you feel most comfortable with now?

## Writing and Discussion Topics

Write about or discuss the following topics.

1. Look back at activity C on page 39 and read the material again. Describe a mural that you have seen and feel is interesting or important. What are the proper places for murals? Does public art have to be approved by government to be acceptable? Are big graffiti murals (done without approval) also art? What is their proper place?

2. Look at the pictures of recent public art pieces on pages 35 and 43. Do you consider the items in these pictures to be art? Is one better than the other? What criteria do you use to decide?

3. Go online and find information about public art in a city not discussed in this unit. Summarize the information and present it to the class. Include your own opinions on whether it really is art and how it benefits or hurts the city.

# Staying Alive

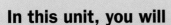

## In this unit, you will

> read about public health, life expectancy, and the impact of vaccination around the world.
> review identifying main ideas vs. supporting details.
> increase your understanding of the target academic words for this unit.

**READING SKILL** Interpreting Charts, Graphs, and Tables

## Self-Assessment

Think about how well you know each target word, and check (✓) the appropriate column. I have...

| TARGET WORDS | never seen the word before | seen the word but am not sure what it means | seen the word and understand what it means | used the word, but am not sure if correctly | used the word confidently in *either* speaking *or* writing | used the word confidently in *both* speaking *and* writing |
|---|---|---|---|---|---|---|
| **AWL** | | | | | | |
| 🔑 approximate | | | | | | |
| 🔑 aspect | | | | | | |
| 🔑 assure | | | | | | |
| compensate | | | | | | |
| 🔑 definite | | | | | | |
| empirical | | | | | | |
| hierarchy | | | | | | |
| isolate | | | | | | |
| 🔑 layer | | | | | | |
| outcome | | | | | | |
| radical | | | | | | |
| 🔑 recover | | | | | | |
| 🔑 resolve | | | | | | |
| straightforward | | | | | | |

🔑 Oxford 3000™ keywords

 **Outside the Reading** What do you know about public health?
Watch the video on the student website to find out more.

## Before You Read

**A.** Answer these questions. Discuss your answers in a small group.

1. Who is the oldest person that you know? How is this person's health?

   _____

   _____

2. What factors do you think have an impact on life expectancy? Rank these factors from *1* (most important) to *10* (least important).

   ___ nutrition

   ___ health

   ___ education

   ___ income

   ___ occupation

   ___ family history

   ___ medical care

   ___ geographic location

   ___ lifestyle

   ___ other: _____

3. If you had lived in a different time in history, do you think you would have reached your current age, or would you have died already? Why?

   _____

   _____

   _____

**B.** This reading contains several graphs and charts. Preview them and predict what the article will be about. Quickly discuss your predictions with a partner.

**MORE WORDS YOU'LL NEED**

**eradicate:** to destroy something (usually a disease) completely

**immunity:** the state of being unaffected by a disease

**immunize:** to protect someone against a disease by giving a vaccine

**life expectancy:** the average number of years a person can expect to live

**mortality:** the number of deaths in a certain period of time or in a certain place

**vaccine:** a substance that is given to people to protect them against a particular disease

# Read

This research report discusses the factors that affect life expectancy.

# The Determinants of Mortality

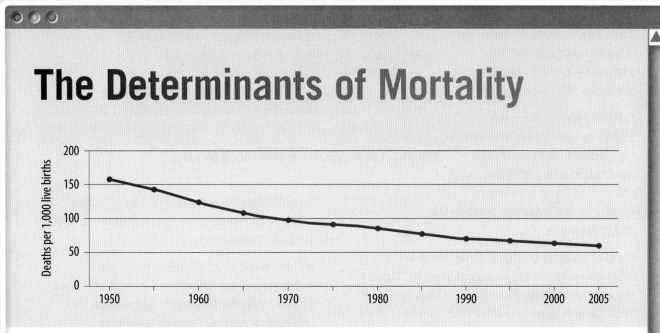

**FIGURE 1.** World Infant Mortality Rates, 1950–2005.  *(Data source: UN)*

For most of human history, life expectancy has been short—**approximately** 25 years for our ancient ancestors, and only 37 years for residents of England in 1700. In just the past
5 century, however, life expectancy has increased by over 30 years.

Dramatic changes began in the 18th century. Life expectancy in England rose to 41 years by 1820, 50 years by the early 20th century,
10 and 78 years today. A similar shift took place in all developed countries. The drop in mortality rates was particularly **radical** among children (Figure 1). This was because of the near eradication of deaths
15 from infectious diseases— formerly the most common cause of death, since the young are most likely to get infections.

The most important **aspects** of
20 daily life that affected mortality reduction were nutrition, public health measures, and medicine.

The history of mortality reduction is spoken of in terms of three
25 phases. In the first phase, from the mid-18th century to the mid-19th century, improved agricultural techniques played a large role. These techniques resulted in increased food supply, better nutrition, and
30 economic growth. Emerging public health measures also played a role at this stage. The second phase ran from the end of the 19th century into the 20th. Public health became more important. People were given advice
35 about personal health practices based on a growing understanding of the causes of disease. Because of high mortality rates in

| | Total Reduction in Mortality Rate 1900–1936 | Share of Total Due to Clean Water |
|---|---|---|
| Typhoid Mortality | 96% | 96%* |
| Total Mortality | 30% | 43% |
| Infant Mortality | 62% | 74% |
| Child Mortality | 81% | 62% |

**FIGURE 2.** Effect of Filtration and Chlorination on Mortality
*Achieved five years after adoption of clean water technologies.

cities, urban centers started to deliver clean water (Figure 2)
40 and remove waste. With the improved water supply, sewage, and general personal hygiene, there was a dramatic reduction in water- and food-borne
45 diseases—typhoid, cholera, dysentery, and tuberculosis.

The third phase, from the 1930s to now, is the time of big medicine. It started with
50 vaccination and antibiotics, and has moved on to a variety of expensive and intensive treatments and procedures.

Looking across countries, there are great
55 differences in life expectancy (Figure 3). There are also sharp differences in who dies and from what. Deaths among children account for **approximately** 30 percent of deaths in poor countries but less than 1 percent of deaths in
60 rich countries. Most deaths in rich countries are from cancers and cardiovascular disease, while most deaths in poor countries are from infectious diseases.

Though differences persist, many poorer countries
65 have recently experienced large improvements in life expectancy. In India and China, life expectancy has risen by 30 years since 1950. Even in Africa, life expectancy rose by 13 years from the early 1950s until the late 1980s, when the spread of
70 HIV/AIDS reversed the trend.

What factors explain this **outcome**? Some of the main factors are changes in income, literacy (especially among women), and the supply of calories. Public health interventions, such as
75 immunization campaigns, improvements in water supply, and the use of antibiotics, have also made a big difference.

Although the connection between economic growth and improved health seems
80 **straightforward**, the **empirical** evidence for this is not completely clear. This may be because urbanization[1] often goes along with growth.

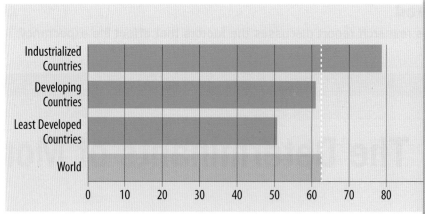

**FIGURE 3.** Life Expectancy at Birth, 2001 (in years)

Growth must be accompanied by effective public health measures in order to bring about
85 mortality reductions.

Within developed countries, there are well-documented differences in mortality rates by race, income, education, occupation, or urban/rural status. There is a **definite**
90 **hierarchy** to healthiness—the higher the socioeconomic status of a group, generally the lower the mortality rate. Some explanations for this include **definite** differences in access to medical care, in access to the resources
95 needed to buy food and shelter, in health-related behaviors such as smoking, and in levels of "psychosocial stress."

The link between social status and health is likely not due to any **isolated** factor. Education,
100 however, seems to have a positive effect on health. This may be due to increased knowledge about health and technology.

Is there a universal theory of mortality that can explain improvements over time, differences
105 across countries, and differences across groups? It can be argued that knowledge, science, and technology are important **aspects** of any logical explanation. As for the future, an increase in the production of new knowledge
110 and treatments is likely to increase inequality in health **outcomes** in the short term. The silver lining,[2] though, is that help is on the way, not only for those who receive it first, but eventually for everyone.

---

[1] *urbanization:* taking on the characteristics of city life
[2] *silver lining:* referring to the expression "every cloud has a silver lining," it is the one good **aspect** of something generally bad.

# Reading Comprehension

Answer the questions below. Look back at Reading 1 as necessary. Then compare your answers with a partner.

1. What has happened to life expectancy in the past 30 years?

   _It has increased._

2. Which age group was affected the most? Why?

   _____

3. What major changes occurred during these time periods?

| Time Period | Change |
|---|---|
| mid-18th to mid-19th century | |
| end of 19th to early 20th century | |
| mid-20th century to now | |

4. According to Reading 1, which of these factors positively affect life expectancy? Put a check (✓) next to them. Be prepared to explain your choices.

   ___infectious diseases          ___ warm climate

   ___better nutrition             ___ intense medical treatments

   ___young parents                ___ living in a city

   ___many doctors in the community ___ antibiotics

   ___clean water                  ___ lower socioeconomic status

5. What does the article predict for the future of health outcomes?

   _____

   _____

# READING SKILL     Interpreting Charts, Graphs, and Tables

## LEARN

Charts, graphs, and tables provide vital information and support the information in a text. By presenting information graphically, the reader can see trends and patterns more easily.

People often refer to graphic information as *charts*, regardless of their actual type (chart, graph, table, etc). In academic texts, however, graphic information is usually cited as a *figure*, as in Reading 1. Sometimes, an author will cite figures and tables separately.

## APPLY

**A.   Match the chart from Reading 1 with its topic.**

   ___ 1. Figure 1          a. effects of water purification

   ___ 2. Figure 2          b. life expectancy at birth

   ___ 3. Figure 3          c. world infant mortality rates

**B.** With a partner, discuss the charts in Reading 1 by answering these questions.

Figure 1: What general trend can you see? What do you expect to happen in the future, based on this information?

Figure 2: What percentage of reduction in infant mortality is a result of clean water? What conclusions can you draw about clean water and mortality rate?

Figure 3: Which region has the lowest life expectancy at birth? Which region has the highest? What is surprising or interesting to you in this chart? Based on this chart, how long can you expect to live? Do you agree with the prediction? Why or why not?

## Vocabulary Activities | STEP I: Word Level

**A.** Scan Reading 1 for these target vocabulary words and match them with their definitions. Use a dictionary to help you.

___ 1. radical            a. an end result; consequence

___ 2. aspect           b. easy to understand, simple

___ 3. approximately     c. very great, extreme

___ 4. outcome         d. certain, without doubt

___ 5. straightforward     e. not quite exact or correct

___ 6. empirical         f. solitary; alone

___ 7. definite          g. a distinct feature or element

___ 8. isolated         h. based on experiments or practical experience, not ideas

The words *radical* (adjective) and *radically* (adverb) are used to describe changes in something. The noun *radical* means "a person who wants great social or political changes."

CORPUS

**B.** Complete these sentences with the correct form of *radical*.

1. There were _____*radical*_____ changes in life expectancy with the introduction of clean water.

2. The life expectancy of infants changed _____ with the use of vaccinations.

3. In the early days of vaccination, some doctors were considered _____ for supporting the idea of mass immunization.

4. The aspect of public health that has most _____ affected people's lives is clean water.

5. The spread of HIV/AIDS has made a _____ difference in public health policy around the world.

The word *aspect* refers to one of the qualities or parts of a situation, idea, or problem. It takes the preposition *of.*

> One **aspect** <u>of</u> a person's socioeconomic status is income level.

CORPUS

**C.** What are some aspects of these situations that a person should consider before making a decision? Discuss with a partner.

1. deciding which college to attend
2. deciding on a career path
3. choosing a movie to watch with a friend
4. choosing a movie to watch with your mother
5. making vacation plans
6. renting an apartment

## Vocabulary Activities   STEP II: Sentence Level

**D.** Which of these things is straightforward? Do any of them have aspects that are straightforward but are not straightforward as a whole? Discuss your answers in a small group. Give examples to support your ideas.

1. buying a used car
2. communicating with your boss
3. going to the doctor
4. picking up a package
5. doing homework
6. trading music with a friend

| Word Form Chart | | | |
|---|---|---|---|
| **Noun** | **Verb** | **Adjective** | **Adverb** |
| approximation | approximate | approximate | approximately |
| definiteness | _____ | definite | definitely |
| isolation | isolate | isolated | _____ |

**E.** Read the information about the effects of clean water on public health. In your notebook, restate each sentence using the word in parentheses. Discuss your sentences with a partner or in a small group.

1. At the start of the 20th century, high mortality rates were common, specifically in urban areas. Yet by the mid-1900s, these rates had dropped, with life expectancy rising in developed nations. (*isolated, definite*)

   *Early in the 20th century, high mortality rates were somewhat **isolated** in urban areas, but by the mid-1900s there was a **definite** drop and people were living much longer in developed nations.*

2. The introduction of a plentiful supply of clean water in major cities accounted for roughly half of the 30 percent decline in urban death rates during the early 1900s. (*approximately* or *approximate*)

3. Clean water was, without a doubt, one of the most significant causes of rapid health improvements at the beginning of the 20th century. (*definitely*)

4. Researchers began focusing on the role of clean water alone, after they discovered that deaths dropped sharply in cities that filtered their drinking water. (*isolate* or *isolated*)

**F.** Rewrite this sentence two ways, using the form of *approximate* indicated.

Clean water was responsible for cutting about three-quarters of deaths and nearly two-thirds of child mortality in the first 40 years of the 20th century.

1. approximate (*adjective*)

_____

_____

_____

_____

2. approximately

_____

_____

_____

_____

A *hierarchy* is "a system of organization that has many grades or ranks from the lowest to the highest." The adjective form is *hierarchical*.

> I prefer to work in a cooperative setting, with people at my level. I don't want to be in a **hierarchical** organization with lots of bosses.

CORPUS

**G.** What do you think is the hierarchy in each of these situations? Rank the people from most important (1) to least important (5) in each case. Discuss your hierarchies in a small group. In what other situations have you noticed hierarchies?

a. School

___ teacher

___ principal/director

___ older students

___ my class

___ new students

b. Health center

___ doctor

___ nurse

___ patient

___ technicians

___ clerks

c. Family

___ mother

___ me

___ grandparents

___ siblings

___ father

## Before You Read

**A.** Read these questions. Discuss your answers in a small group.

1. What are some common childhood diseases? Did you have any of them?

2. Do you know which vaccines you received as a child? If so, what were they for? How were they delivered (by mouth, by injection, etc.)? If you remember the experience, what was it like? Were you scared? Did it hurt?

3. Imagine that a drug company develops a vaccine that it says will protect against all major diseases. They need volunteers to test the vaccine. Would you volunteer? Why or why not?

**B.** Preview the tables in Reading 2. What do you think this text will discuss? Compare your ideas with a partner.

## Read

This report from the World Health Organization recounts the positive effect that immunizations have had around the world.

# Immunization against Diseases of Public Health Importance

### THE BENEFITS OF IMMUNIZATION

Vaccines—which protect against disease by **assuring** immunity—are widely and routinely given around the world. This practice is based on the idea that it is better to keep people from 5 falling ill than to focus only on helping them **recover** once they are ill. Suffering, disability, and death are avoided. Immunization is thought to prevent two to three million childhood deaths each year. In addition, infection is reduced, 10 strain on health-care systems is eased, and money is frequently saved that can be used for other health services.

Immunization is a proven tool for controlling and even eradicating disease. An immunization 15 campaign carried out by the World Health Organization (WHO) from 1967 to 1977 eradicated the natural occurrence of smallpox.

When the program began, the disease still threatened 60% of the world's population and 20 killed every fourth victim. Eradication of poliomyelitis is within reach. Since the launch by WHO and its partners of the Global Polio Eradication Initiative in 1988, infections have fallen by 99%, and about five million people 25 have escaped paralysis. Between 2000 and 2008, measles deaths dropped worldwide by almost 78%, and some regions have **resolved** to eliminate the disease.

### GLOBAL IMMUNIZATION COVERAGE

Coverage has greatly increased since WHO's 30 Expanded Program on Immunization began in 1974, and the results are encouraging (Table 1). In 2009, global DTP3 (three doses of the diphtheria-tetanus-pertussis combination vaccine) coverage was 82%—up from 20% in 1980. However, millions of children worldwide were not reached by DTP3 in 2009, including many in South Asia and sub-Saharan Africa.

**TABLE 1.**

| Annual deaths* in 2002 from vaccine-preventable diseases | | | |
|---|---|---|---|
| Disease | Under 5 | Over 5 | Total |
| Diphtheria | 4,000 | 1,000 | 5,000 |
| Measles | 540,000 | 70,000 | 610,000 |
| Polio | _____ | _____ | 1,000 |
| Tetanus | 198,000 | 15,000 | 213,000 |
| Pertussis | 294,000 | _____ | 294,000 |
| Hepatitis B | _____ | 600,000 | 600,000 |
| Haemophilus influenzae b (Hib) | 386,000 | _____ | 386,000 |
| Yellow fever | 15,000 | 15,000 | 30,000 |
| **TOTAL** | **1,437,000** | **701,000** | **2,138,000** |

*WHO Estimates (January 2005)*

## NEW VACCINES

Numerous new vaccines with major potential for improving health in developing countries have been produced since 2002. Incidence of meningitis, rotavirus, and pneumococcal disease, which killed millions of children annually (Table 2), has fallen in areas where the new vaccines have been introduced.

**TABLE 2.**

| Annual deaths in 2002 from diseases for which vaccines are now available | | | |
|---|---|---|---|
| Disease | Under 5 | Over 5 | Total |
| Meningitis AC* | 10,000 | 16,000 | 26,000 |
| Rotavirus* | 402,000 | 47,000 | 449,000 |
| Pneumococcal Disease* | 716,000 | 897,000 | 1,612,000 |
| **TOTAL** | **1,128,000** | **960,000** | **2,087,000** |

*WHO Estimates (January 2005)*

## HISTORY

Introducing a small amount of smallpox virus by inhaling through the nose or by making a number of small pricks through the **layers** of skin (variolation) to create resistance to the disease began in the 10th or 11th century in Central Asia. Variolation was introduced into England in 1721. There, in 1798, Edward Jenner began treatments against smallpox, the first systematic effort to control a disease through immunization.

In 1885, Louis Pasteur developed the first vaccine to protect humans against rabies. Vaccines against diphtheria and tetanus were introduced in the early 1900s, the Calmette-Guérin vaccine (against tuberculosis) in 1927, the Salk polio vaccine in 1955, and vaccines against measles and mumps in the 1960s.

## HOW VACCINES WORK

Vaccines typically provide the immune system with harmless copies of an *antigen:* a portion of the surface of a bacterium or virus that the immune system recognizes as "foreign." A vaccine may also provide a non-active version of a toxin—a poison produced by a bacterium—so that the body can create a defense against it.

Once an antigen is noticed by the immune system, white blood cells called B-lymphocytes create a protein called an antibody that is designed to attach to that antigen. Many copies of this antibody are produced. If a true infection of the same disease occurs, still more antibodies are created, and as they attach to their targets they may block the activity of the virus or bacterial strain directly, thus fighting infection. In addition, once in place, the antibodies make it much easier for other parts of the immune system to recognize and destroy the invading agent.

Immune systems are designed to "remember." Once exposed to a particular bacterium or virus, they retain immunity against it for years, decades, or even a lifetime. This means they are prepared to quickly defeat a later infection. This is a huge benefit because a body encountering a germ for the first time may need from seven to twelve days to effectively defend it, and by then serious illness and even death may occur.

## EFFECTIVENESS AND SAFETY

All vaccines used for routine immunization are
95 very effective in preventing disease, although no vaccine attains 100% effectiveness. More than one dose of a vaccine is generally given to increase the chance of developing immunity.

Vaccines are very safe, and side effects
100 are minor—especially when compared with the diseases they are designed to prevent. Serious complications occur rarely. For example, severe allergic reactions result at a rate of one for every 100,000 doses of measles vaccine. Two to four
105 cases of vaccine-associated paralytic polio have been reported for every one million children receiving oral polio vaccine.

## COST-EFFECTIVENESS OF IMMUNIZATION

Immunization is considered among the most cost-effective of health investments. There is

110 a well-defined target group; contact with the health system is only needed at the time of delivery; and vaccination does not require any major change of lifestyle.

A recent study estimated that if the
115 coverage for the pneumococcal disease vaccine reached the levels of DTP3 coverage in Latin America and the Caribbean, it would prevent over half of all cases of the disease and about 9,500 deaths annually. This
120 could be achieved at a cost of as low as 62 U.S. dollars per life saved. The cost of the immunizations is clearly **compensated** for by its life-saving value.

## THE DECADE OF VACCINES

The effort to increase immunization coverage
125 around the world is continuing with the Global Vaccine Action Plan. This plan promotes the discovery and development of vaccines as well as their delivery to the world's poorest countries. The aim is to prevent the deaths of
130 millions of children over the next decade.

## Reading Comprehension

**A.** Mark each sentence as *T* (true) or *F* (false) according to the information in Reading 2. In your notebook, cite the location of the information by line number, and correct each false statement.

___ 1. Vaccines protect against suffering, disability, and death.

___ 2. Smallpox has been eradicated through immunization.

___ 3. Variolation first began in West Africa.

___ 4. The first vaccine was developed to protect humans against rabies.

___ 5. There is no problem reaching all of the children worldwide with immunizations.

___ 6. Once immune systems are exposed to a bacterium or virus, they "remember" it and can easily fight against an infection later.

___ 7. Side effects and serious complications from vaccines occur frequently.

___ 8. Immunization is extremely expensive and not very cost effective.

**B.** Use the tables in Reading 2 to complete these sentences.

1. _One thousand_ deaths were caused by polio in 2002.

2. The disease _____ caused the same number of deaths in people under five and over five in 2002.

3. _____ caused the most total deaths in 2002.

4. _____ killed more people over five years old than small children.

5. _____ deaths from meningitis in 2002 could have been prevented if there was a vaccine.

6. The vaccine for rotavirus will have the most effect on people who are _____ .

---

**REVIEW A SKILL** Identifying Main Ideas vs. Supporting Details (See p. 20)

In your notebook, create an outline of the article using the main ideas and supporting details from each section.

---

**READING SKILL** Interpreting Charts, Graphs, and Tables

### LEARN

Another type of chart is called a *pie chart*. It is used to show how one thing or group of things is divided.

### APPLY

**A.** Study this example of a pie chart and answer the questions below in your notebook.

**Vaccine-Preventable Diseases**

In 2002, WHO estimated that 1.4 million deaths among children under five years were due to diseases that could have been prevented by routine vaccination.

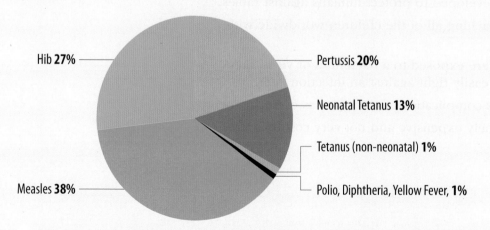

Hib **27%**
Pertussis **20%**
Neonatal Tetanus **13%**
Tetanus (non-neonatal) **1%**
Polio, Diphtheria, Yellow Fever, **1%**
Measles **38%**

1. What percentage of children who died from preventable diseases died from Hib?

2. What was the most common preventable disease that killed children?

3. How many actual deaths were caused by Pertussis?

**B.** Read this paragraph about a polio outbreak. Then create a chart, graph, table, or pie chart in your notebook depicting some or all of the information. Discuss your chart in a small group.

Although the incidence of polio has been reduced worldwide by 99% since 1988, outbreaks are still occurring in some areas, particularly when the vaccination program is not kept up. A recent outbreak in West Africa spread from Nigeria, where there were 798 cases in 2008. That year, there was 1 case in Côte d'Ivoire, and 6 in Benin, but no cases in Mauritania, Sierra Leone, Liberia and Cameroon. In 2009, the number of cases in Nigeria fell to 388, but the outbreak had spread. Côte d'Ivore had 26 cases, Benin had 20, Mauritania had 13, Sierra Leone and Liberia had 11, and Cameroon had 3.

## Vocabulary Activities  STEP I: Word Level

**A.** Read these facts about the eradication of smallpox. Then complete the sentences using the target vocabulary in the box.

| | | | |
|---|---|---|---|
| approximately | isolated | outcome | recovered |
| assured | layers | radical | resolved |
| definite | | | |

1. During the 15th century, an early form of smallpox vaccination was practiced in China and other parts of the world. Healthy people were intentionally infected through the _____ of skin with substances from the pustules of people suffering from smallpox.

2. Later, in the 18th century, this practice was adopted in England, where smallpox was the most common disease, causing _____ 20% of all deaths in London. An expression of the times was, "Mothers counted their children only after they had had the smallpox."

3. An English doctor, Edward Jenner, created the first vaccine in 1796. Dr. Jenner had heard that dairymaids, _____ from other people in the countryside, often had cowpox, a milder disease related to smallpox.

4. After the dairymaids _____ from cowpox, they were immune to smallpox. Jenner _____ to find out why.

5. Jenner performed the first vaccination on a boy with material taken from lesions of cowpox. The _____ was that the boy, and all people who received the vaccine later, were immune to smallpox.

6. In the 19th century, vaccination laws were established in Europe and the United States. These laws _____ people that vaccination was safe, and they began to be vaccinated against smallpox routinely. In the 20th century, vaccination against smallpox became a worldwide effort.

7. The last _____ case of smallpox in the United States was reported in 1949, and routine vaccination of children in the United States ended in 1971. The last case of smallpox in the world was in Ethiopia in 1976.

8. In 1980, scientists announced that the once _____ idea of vaccines had been successful at eradicating smallpox from the world.

To *assure* means "to promise somebody something will certainly happen or will be true, especially if he/she is worried."

> The doctor **assured** us this vaccination is perfectly safe.

**B.** What might each of these people want to *assure* someone of? Discuss your ideas in a small group.

1. a teenager to a parent
2. a student to a teacher
3. a friend to another friend
4. a husband to a wife
5. an employer to an employee

## Vocabulary Activities  STEP II: Sentence Level

The verb *resolve* has two definitions. It can mean "to find a solution to a problem" or "to decide something and be determined not to change your mind."

> Most of the difficulties have been **resolved**.

> Ray **resolved** never to let that same thing happen again.

The noun *resolve* means "a strong determination to achieve something."

> The difficulties in her way merely strengthened her **resolve**.

There is another noun form as well. *Resolution* is more formal and refers to a firm decision to do or not to do something.

> The United Nations passed a **resolution** to eradicate polio around the world.

**C.** Read these reasons why immunization is a cost-effective public health policy. In your notebook, restate each one using a form of the word *resolve*. Be prepared to read aloud or discuss your sentences in a small group or with the class.

1. By preventing disease, immunization allows countries to reduce the amount of money spent on treatment and hospitalization costs.

   *If countries resolve to prevent disease through immunization, less money will be used on medical treatment or hospitalization.*

2. Immunization helps national governments avoid the expense of treating major outbreaks of disease and the loss of productivity that comes with these illnesses.

3. Immunization also increases productivity by allowing parents to work instead of staying home to care for sick children.

4. It costs just 17 U.S. dollars to immunize a child with the six core vaccines: polio, diphtheria, pertussis, measles, tetanus, and tuberculosis.

5. Most immunizations cost less than 50 U.S. dollars per healthy life year saved.

**D.** Review each section of Reading 2. Write 2–3 sentences in your notebook that summarize the main idea of each section. Use the target vocabulary in parentheses in your summaries.

1. the benefits of immunization (*assure, resolve*)
2. global immunization coverage (*definite*)
3. new vaccines (*approximate*)
4. history (*layers*)
5. how vaccines work (*recover*)
6. effectiveness and safety (*aspect*)
7. the cost-effectiveness of immunization (*compensate*)

To *compensate* means "to remove or reduce the bad effect of something" or "to make up for something."

> He **compensated** for his lack of money by doing most of the work himself.

As a noun, *compensation* can refer to the money that you pay to somebody or to something that removes or reduces the bad effect of something.

> Some companies provide a shuttle bus to the nearest train station as part of employee **compensation**.

> The owner of the property had to pay **compensation** to the woman who slipped on his stairs and broke her leg.

CORPUS

**E.** What sort of compensation (if any) should the people get in each situation? Discuss your ideas in a small group. Then choose one situation and write a paragraph in your notebook explaining your opinion. Be prepared to read your work aloud to the class.

1. Your son is riding his bicycle in a city park. He loses control for a moment and goes onto the grass. He hits a hole in the ground and is thrown from his bike, breaking his arm and ruining the bike.

2. Your friend has bought tickets to a sold-out concert of your favorite musician. You decide to take a nap before the show but sleep too long. The concert is half over by the time you wake up.

3. Your family is moving to a new apartment and there is a lot of mess and confusion. Your parents are stressed out and very busy. So busy, in fact, that they have clearly forgotten that today is your birthday.

**F.** Self-Assessment Review: Go back to page 49 and reassess your knowledge of the target vocabulary. How has your understanding of the words changed? What words do you feel most comfortable with now?

## Writing and Discussion Topics

Write about or discuss the following topics.

1. Go online and research some of the arguments against immunization. Summarize them and give your own opinion on the subject.

2. It has been argued that clean water has had the single most important impact in public health and the eradication of disease. What do you predict will be the next great step in public health or the next great medical discovery?

3. Diseases like smallpox have been eradicated, and common viruses that cause the flu have been controlled, but there is still the possibility a deadly disease or virus could occur in our lifetime. What can governments do to prepare for such a global health risk?

# UNIT 5

# Bodies in Motion

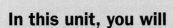

## In this unit, you will

> read about the latest developments in photographic motion studies conducted for science, industry, medicine, athletics, and art.

> review identifying main ideas vs. supporting details.

> increase your understanding of the target academic words for this unit.

**READING SKILL** Summarizing a Text Using Nontext Elements

## Self-Assessment

Think about how well you know each target word, and check (✓) the appropriate column. I have…

| TARGET WORDS | never seen the word before | seen the word but am not sure what it means | seen the word and understand what it means | used the word, but am not sure if correctly | used the word confidently in *either* speaking *or* writing | used the word confidently in *both* speaking *and* writing |
|---|---|---|---|---|---|---|
| **AWL** | | | | | | |
| abstract | | | | | | |
| 🔑 appreciate | | | | | | |
| 🔑 available | | | | | | |
| 🔑 display | | | | | | |
| 🔑 drama | | | | | | |
| 🔑 encounter | | | | | | |
| 🔑 expose | | | | | | |
| hence | | | | | | |
| 🔑 image | | | | | | |
| 🔑 restore | | | | | | |
| sequence | | | | | | |
| 🔑 series | | | | | | |
| transit | | | | | | |
| 🔑 version | | | | | | |
| 🔑 visible | | | | | | |

🔑 Oxford 3000™ keywords

## Before You Read

**Read these questions. Discuss your answers in a small group.**

1. How do you assess your own performance in sports, or another physical activity (dance, aerobics, etc.)?

2. Do you like the slow-motion replays of important moments in a sports program? Why or why not? What is the point of them?

3. Have you ever seen video of your performance? If so, was it helpful? How? If not, do you think it would be helpful? How?

## Read

The first selection was adapted from the "Collision Detection" column of the online magazine *Slate*. The second selection was adapted from press releases by BBC Sport and the websites of Dartfish and its American partner, Sportvision.

# THE DARTFISH OLYMPICS

StroMotion™ shows frame by frame action.

### POSTED BY: CLIVE THOMPSON, AUGUST 24, 10:55 A.M.

If you've watched the most recent summer and winter Olympics, you've probably seen StroMotion™—the photo software that breaks an athlete's fluid movements into stop-motion-
5 style freeze-frames. This fascinating software is made by the Swiss company Dartfish, and apparently Olympians have been using it to train in an incredibly innovative way. They use film footage of the performance of a past Olympic
10 athlete and **display** it alongside footage of themselves. Both **sequences** are broken down into StroMotion™ frames.

As the Associated Press reports, pole vault star Toby Stevenson used Dartfish to virtually
15 "compete against" a video of Sergey Bubka, the world record holder.

"I used it until smoke came out of the machine. It's great," said Stevenson, who won the silver medal in the 2004 Olympic men's pole vaulting
20 event. Stevenson could review his practice jumps on a laptop within seconds. Within two hours of a track meet, he was able to watch himself on an LCD projector back at the hotel. Or he had his day's work burned onto a CD.

25 While Stevenson's muscles told him one thing, the digital video might **display** something else.

"It was a big reason for my success," Stevenson said. "I made a jump, and between every jump I watched my jump, and after practice I watched
30 every jump on Dartfish."

This reminds me of the idea of the "ghost" competition in many popular video games. I first **encountered** it in the original Mario Kart back in 1996: You could race around a track and then do it
35 again, competing against a recorded, "ghost," **version** of yourself. Competing against your ghost—or that of a world-ranked competitor—is now a pretty common thing in many games. It reminds me of how game innovations have constantly pioneered
40 techniques that are transforming how we view, and play, real-world sports.

There is some debate about whether this is a good thing. Some famous judges—such as Cynthia Potter, a well-known diving analyst—wonder
45 whether StroMotion™ is harming the sport. When judges use it, it might encourage them to give demerits[1] for things they normally wouldn't see.

"With the naked eye, you don't see these tiny little things that might be called deductions,"
50 says Potter, as divers lined up for midday practice plunges[2] at an Olympic venue. "I don't know if you'd even need judges if you could program all this into a computer."

But, she continues, "Human judges allow for
55 artistic judgment—and allow divers to put personality in their dives."

Of course, this isn't an entirely new thing. The photo finish has been around for decades in many sports—and has caused huge
60 controversies in everything from the 100-meter dash to car racing. Modern media are likely to make things even stranger. I can easily envision the next few Olympics, since Dartfish has released a program for use on
65 mobile devices. I imagine fans getting personalized StroMotion™ streams sent to their mobile phones, which they can view and then vote on which athlete did the best dive.

# BBC SPORT USES STROMOTION™ TECHNIQUE

BBC Sport is a leader in sports broadcasting innovation and was the first network in British television to use the StroMotion™ technique.

StroMotion™ is an **image** enhancement
5 technique. It creates stunning video footage **displaying** the evolution of an athlete's movement, technique, execution, and tactics over space and time.

**Sports competition and viewing is being changed by StroMotion™.**

Television sports viewers are able to see
10 an athletic movement, such as the line of a skier, unfold before their eyes by compounding video **images** into a frame-by-frame **sequence**. The StroMotion™ concept is based on stroboscoping, a means to analyze
15 rapid movement so that a moving object is perceived as a **series** of static **images** along the object's trajectory.[3]

StroMotion™ special effects add particular value to winter sports. For example, the StroMotion™
20 technique applied to an ice skater during a jump allows us to clearly see the technique and quality of its execution by highlighting the maneuver—the preparation phase, the elevation progression, the inclination and
25 straightness of the body, and the quality and speed of execution.

---

[1] *demerits:* points against something that is being judged
[2] *plunges:* sudden, forceful falls or dives into something
[3] *trajectory:* the path of something in motion

Applied to the half-pipe[4] events in gravity-extreme sports such as snowboarding, skateboarding, and skiing, StroMotion™ allows viewers to fully
30 **appreciate** the technique and the quality of aerial maneuvers (spontaneity,[5] elevation, landing) and highlights the different phases and their **transitions**.

The StroMotion™ technology is worldwide patent-
35 protected and is exclusively **available** from Dartfish products and services. Among these products is another unique patented video application called SimulCam™.

With SimulCam™, whenever two athletes are
40 competing at different times but over the same terrain (skiers, for example), their filmed performances can be combined into a single video. This video shows both competitors appearing to compete together. SimulCam™
45 pictures show the relative position, speed, and posture of the two competitors at each instant in a single **display**, allowing for a direct side-by-side comparison of athletic performances. SimulCam™'s value for
50 professional commentary at televised athletic events is much **appreciated** by experts, especially for purposes of comparing performance styles and visualizing time differences. It illustrates what one tenth of a
55 second's difference can mean in competition. This technology is used in a variety of sports, but it is particularly **dramatic** to watch during the Olympics. There, tiny flaws made **visible** can keep a competitor off the medal stand.

---

[4] *half-pipe:* a U-shaped, high-sided ramp
[5] *spontaneity:* unplanned action arising from a momentary impulse

## Reading Comprehension

Mark each sentence as *T* (true) or *F* (false) according to the information in Reading 1. Correct each false statement on the line below it.

___ 1. Using StroMotion™ and SimulCam™, it's possible for an Olympic athlete to observe his or her technique and compare it with that of a champion from the past.

___ 2. The Olympic athlete Toby Stevenson sometimes feels he has made a good jump, but the StroMotion™ doesn't always confirm this.

___ 3. Some diving analysts don't like StroMotion™ replays because they don't take into account a diver's creativity and artistry.

___ 4. StroMotion™ is the first photographic technique to cause controversy in sports.

___ 5. Clive Thompson predicts that the viewers themselves might soon be voting on Olympic dives after watching them on their cell phones.

___ 6. StroMotion™ would probably be useful in viewing any sport that involves jumping.

___ 7. StroMotion™ is of no value in viewing summer sports.

___ 8. Many different companies sell StroMotion™ technology.

___ 9. The images made visible by SimulCam™ technology help viewers appreciate tiny differences in athletic style and performance time.

___10. SimulCam™ provides useful displays in various sports but adds little to our appreciation of the Olympics.

## READING SKILL   Summarizing a Text Using Nontext Elements

### LEARN

The task of summarizing a text can be broken down into two steps:
- Figure out the central ideas of a selection.
- Combine them briefly and clearly.

Also be sure to include the nontext elements—such as pictures, tables, charts, and graphs—in your summary.

### APPLY

1. Identify two main ideas in *The Dartfish Olympics*.

2. Identify two main ideas in *BBC Sport Uses StroMotion™ Technique*.

3. Look at the photos that accompany Reading 1. How do they link to the main ideas? Consider the photos on their own. What main idea do they present?

4. Combine the main ideas from 1, 2, and 3 above into a summary of Reading 1. One or two sentences should be enough.

**A.** Put each word in the box in the correct column, based on which target word it is a synonym for. Use your dictionary to check the meanings of new words.

| | | | |
|---|---|---|---|
| accessible | obtainable | treasure | usable |
| advertised | show | understand | value |
| exhibit | | | |

| available | display | appreciate |
|---|---|---|
| _____ | _____ | _____ |
| _____ | _____ | _____ |
| _____ | _____ | _____ |

| Word Form Chart | | | |
|---|---|---|---|
| **Noun** | **Verb** | **Adjective** | **Adverb** |
| appreciation | appreciate | appreciative appreciated unappreciated | appreciatively |

*Appreciate*, as a transitive verb, takes an object and means:

| to value | The ex-prisoners **appreciated** their freedom. |
|---|---|
| to be thankful for | We really **appreciated** his help. |
| to understand the significance of something | I can **appreciate** why this is such a big problem for you. |

Note: As an intransitive verb, *appreciate* does not take an object and means "to increase in value over time." It is a very common word in business and art. The opposite is *depreciate*.

> The property they bought last year has already **appreciated** 25 percent.

> The value of a new car **depreciates** as soon as you buy it.

**B.** Complete the sentences with the correct form of *appreciate* from the chart above.

1. Her favorite courses in high school were in art and music _____ .

2. My friend was very _____ when we gave him a going-away party.

3. His art collection _____ greatly over a period of 40 years.

4. Their gift to us was very thoughtful and much _____ .

5. Because they are so rare, the old coins have _____ in value.

**C.** Which of these things do you value most? Rank them from *1* (most appreciated) to *6* (least appreciated). Discuss your choices with a partner.

___ your mother's advice      ___ your cell phone

___ quiet neighbors      ___ air conditioning

___ mass transit      ___ privacy

**D.** Which of these things does an adult appreciate better than a child? Write *A* for things adults appreciate, *C* for things children better appreciate, or *B* for things both groups can appreciate equally. Discuss your choices with a partner.

___ the value of sleep      ___ the taste of chocolate

___ the importance of family      ___ a surprise birthday party

___ a good joke      ___ kindness

## Vocabulary Activities    STEP II: Sentence Level

An *image* has both concrete and abstract meanings, but they all connect to the idea of a picture of something.

> The **images** on the screen reminded him of the town where he grew up.
>
> The **image** of the building was beautifully reflected in the lake.
>
> Many people have the **image** of Canada as being cold all the time.
>
> Ads try to create a positive **image** of a product.

The verb *imagine* and the noun *imagination* also come from the word *image*.

There are many expressions and collocations that feature the word *image*.

> She <u>is the very image of</u> her sister.    (She looks exactly like her sister.)
>
> He <u>is the very image of</u> sophistication.    (He has all the qualities of sophistication.)
>
> She <u>is the spitting image of</u> her father.    (She looks and acts like her father.)

CORPUS

**E.** Match each use of the word *image* with the field to which it typically belongs. Then, write an example sentence for each context. Discuss your sentences in a small group.

___ 1. art      a. the public personality or character presented by a person

___ 2. psychology      b. a symbol or metaphor that represents something else

___ 3. business/marketing      c. a duplication of the visual form of a person or object

___ 4. literature      d. an advertising concept conveyed to the public

*Psychology: As role models for young people, pop stars should maintain a healthy, responsible image.*

_____

_____

**F.** The word *version* is very common in the software and publishing industries. Complete the example sentences with the correct term from the box. Then write a new example sentence for each term. Use your dictionary as necessary. Be prepared to read aloud or discuss your new sentences in class.

| | | |
|---|---|---|
| a. electronic version | c. original version | e. standard version |
| b. latest version | d. revised version | f. updated version |

1. For a home computer, the _e___ of the program is usually good enough.
   *The standard version of this program has all the basic tools a student needs.*

2. Some of the information in this manual is old. They need to put out an _____ .

   _____

3. I found some earlier drafts of the proposal, but I need to see the _____ of it.

   _____

4. There were some mistakes in the book, but they were all corrected in the _____ .

   _____

5. You can buy a newspaper at the coffee shop or read the _____ online.

   _____

6. The remake of that movie was okay, but I prefer the _____ .

   _____

**G.** Discuss these questions in a small group.

1. Are you the spitting image of someone in your family? Who? In what ways are you like each other?

2. Do you know someone who is the spitting image of someone else? Who?

3. Who or what would you describe as

   the very image of success

   the very image of beauty

   the very image of elegance

   the very image of evil

   the very image of power

   the very image of fun

**H.** Choose one item from question 3 in activity G and in your notebook write a paragraph about your choice. Be prepared to read your paragraph aloud and discuss your opinions.

## Before You Read

Read these questions. Discuss your answers in a small group.

1. When a horse gallops, do you think all four hooves ever leave the ground at the same time? Why or why not?

2. What does a splash look like? Describe a splash of water or a raindrop as it hits the ground. What happens?

3. Have you ever seen an electronic strobe light in action? Where? In what situation or for what function?

## Read

This article from a popular science magazine is about the history of sequential photography.

# Freeze Frames–Stopping Time

An example of Muybridge's fast-motion photography

For most people, the arc of their golf swing or tennis stroke is an **abstract image**, something that happens much too fast for the unaided eye to see. Fortunately,
5 modern athletes have a special tool **available**—StroMotion™—with which to obtain and study an actual, **visible** record of their movements. But StroMotion™ is not a brand new concept—in fact it's an old idea newly linked to digital
10 video and computer software. StroMotion™ uses processes and technology developed by photographic pioneers such as Eadweard Muybridge, who conducted the first photographic **sequential** motion studies, and
15 Harold Edgerton, inventor of the strobe light, which seems to stop even the speediest objects—like bullets—in **transit**.

In 1872, Leland Stanford—the soon-to-be Governor of California who was also a
20 businessman, horse lover, racetrack owner, and later founder of Stanford University—**encountered** this commonly debated question of the time: whether during a horse's gallop all four hooves were ever off the ground at the
25 same time. This was called "unsupported **transit**," and Stanford took it upon himself to settle this popular debate scientifically. He hired a well-known British photographer named Eadweard Muybridge, then working in San
30 Francisco, to get the answer.

By 1878, Muybridge had successfully photographed a horse in fast motion using a **series** of fifty cameras. The cameras were arranged along a track parallel to the horse's,
35 and each of the camera shutters was triggered by electronic timers developed specifically for the project. The resulting **series** of photos proved that the hooves do all leave the ground at the same time—although not with the legs
40 fully extended forward and back, as artists of

the day had imagined, but rather at the moment when all the hooves are tucked under the horse, as it switches from "pulling" from the front legs to "pushing" from the back legs.

45 Muybridge continued to use this technique to photograph human beings and animals in order to "freeze" and study their motion. He made sequential motion studies of athletes in a wide variety of sports and additional studies of
50 everyday people performing mundane movements like walking down stairs. Muybridge's work helped inaugurate the modern science of biomechanics, the research and analysis of the mechanics of living organisms.

55 Furthermore, when a viewer flips rapidly through a **sequence** of Muybridge's pictures, it appears to the eye that the original motion has been **restored**. Viewers **appreciated** these **images** for reasons of both science and
60 entertainment, and inventors like Thomas Edison were inspired to work harder on the creation of a motion picture process. **Hence** Muybridge is considered to have been a crucial figure in the development of movies.

65 Muybridge showed that the value of a **sequence** of photographs could be greater than that of any single **image**, a lesson that was later applied in photojournalism as well as biomechanics. But after Muybridge, inventors
70 persisted in seeking ways to photograph faster and faster motion, and eventually they came back to the stroboscope.

A stroboscope, also known as a strobe, is an instrument used to make a fast-moving object
75 appear to be slow-moving or stationary.[1] It is mainly employed in industry for the study of the motion of objects, such as rotating machine parts or vibrating strings.

The stroboscope was designed by Joseph
80 Plateau of Belgium in 1832. In its simplest form, it is a rotating disc with evenly spaced small openings cut into it. It is placed between the observer and the moving object and rotates to alternately block and reveal the object. When the
85 speed of the disc is adjusted so that it becomes synchronized[2] with the object's movement, the object seems to slow and stop. The illusion is commonly known as the "stroboscopic effect."

In 1931, almost exactly one hundred years
90 after Plateau, an engineering professor at the Massachusetts Institute of Technology named Harold Edgerton combined the stroboscope and the camera. He created an electronic **version** of the strobe in which the rotating disc was
95 replaced by a special lamp. The lamp emits brief and rapid flashes of light. The frequency of the flash is adjusted so that it is a fraction of the object's speed. At this point, the object appears to be stationary.

100 Although his original goal was to **display** and study the stresses on moving machine parts otherwise **invisible** to the naked eye, Edgerton later used very short flashes of light as a means of producing **dramatic** still
105 photographs of fast-moving objects in **transit**, such as bullets in flight, hovering hummingbirds, and falling milk drops splashing into a bowl. His camera had no shutter. The film was pulled through
110 continuously as in motion picture cameras— but at much higher speeds—and **exposed** by a stroboscopic flash lasting 1/1,000,000 of a second or less.

Edgerton's invention was the basis for
115 the built-in light flash found in nearly all cameras today. Strobes are also popular as a lighting effect in nightclubs, where they create the appearance of dancing in slow motion. Other common uses are in alarm
120 systems, theatrical lighting (for example, to simulate lightning), and as high-**visibility** navigation lights.

Edgerton produced photographs of fast-moving objects in transit, such as milk drops splashing into a bowl.

---

[1] *stationary:* still, not moving
[2] *synchronized:* matching, in step with

In medicine, stroboscopes are used to view the vocal cords. Both the strobe and the camera are placed inside the patient's neck using a procedure called endoscopy. The patient then hums or speaks into a microphone, which in turn activates the stroboscope. Doctors can see the movement of the vocal cords and diagnose problems.

Strobe technology has also been instrumental in the development of underwater scanning technology—useful in searching the sea bottom for shipwrecks—and is valuable in photographing creatures living in the darkest depths of the ocean. Edgerton worked with the undersea explorer Jacques Cousteau, providing him with underwater stroboscopes.

In addition to having the science, engineering, and business skills to advance strobe lighting commercially, Edgerton is equally **appreciated** for his visual flair. Many of the **dramatic images** he created for science are now found in art museums worldwide. In Edgerton's strobe work, science and art **encounter** one another and find that in some way they serve the same need for exactitude—a goal shared by the athletes who use video StroMotion™ today to improve their competitive performance. ■

## Reading Comprehension

Mark each sentence as *T* (true) or *F* (false) according to the information in Reading 2. Correct each false statement on the line below it.

___ 1. Stanford hired Muybridge to find out whether both wings flap simultaneously when a chicken is flying, but Muybridge switched to studying horses.

_____

___ 2. Muybridge failed to prove conclusively that all four of a horse's hooves do at some point leave the ground at the same time.

_____

___ 3. Before Muybridge made his motion studies, painters had incorrectly portrayed a horse's gallop.

_____

___ 4. Motion picture inventor Thomas Edison was aware of Muybridge's work.

_____

___ 5. Edgerton's electronic strobe light and the built-in flash units in today's cameras are unrelated inventions.

_____

___ 6. Creatures living in the darkest depths of the sea were made visible by Edgerton's strobes.

_____

___ 7. The need for exactness is common to art, science, and athletics.

_____

___ 8. Photographs can expand our world by showing us things we can't normally see.

_____

**APPLY**

1. Identify two main topics in Reading 2.

   _____

   _____

2. Look at the photos that accompany Reading 2. How do they link to the main ideas? Consider the photos as a group. What main idea does the group present?

   _____

   _____

3. Combine the main ideas from the text and the accompanying images into a summary of Reading 2.

   _____

   _____

**REVIEW A SKILL** Identifying Main Ideas vs. Supporting Details (See p. 20)

Reread the article on pages 73–75. As you read each paragraph, think about the author's main purpose. Identify the main ideas and supporting details for each paragraph and write these in your notebook.

## Vocabulary Activities | STEP I: Word Level

**A.** Complete these sentences using the target vocabulary in the box.

| | | | |
|---|---|---|---|
| abstract | dramatist | transition | visibility |
| dramatic | invisible | transitional | |

1. Many believe that the best _____ in English was Shakespeare. He wrote at least 37 plays.

2. When writing an essay, it is important to use a _____ to connect the ideas in one paragraph with those in the next paragraph.

3. A painting without a story or representational image is referred to as _____ art.

4. The observation deck at the top of a tall building provides the best view of a city, but only if there is clear _____ that day.

5. The strong contrast between light and dark in black-and-white films can create quite a _____ effect.

6. Doctors can use a strobe and a powerful lens inside the body to make _____ processes viewable on a computer screen.

7. The office hasn't moved completely to the new location yet. We're still in a _____ phase.

**B.** Put each word in the box in the correct column, based on which target word it is a synonym for. Use your dictionary to check the meanings of new words.

| | | | |
|---|---|---|---|
| bring back | reveal | show | thus |
| consequently | revive | therefore | uncover |
| renovate | | | |

**expose**

_____

_____

_____

**hence**

_____

_____

_____

**restore**

_____

_____

_____

| Word Form Chart | | | |
|---|---|---|---|
| **Noun** | **Verb** | **Adjective** | **Adverb** |
| series | _____ | _____ | _____ |
| sequence | sequence | sequential | sequentially |

The word *series* is both a singular and plural noun. When it has the meaning of "one set" it takes a singular verb. When the meaning is "two or more sets," it takes a plural verb.

> A **series** of lectures is planned for next semester. (singular)

> Two **series** of lectures are planned for next year, one in each semester. (plural)

The words *series* and *sequence* are synonyms. *Series* generally refers to "a number of things that come one after another and are of the same type or connected," as in *a series of days* or *a television series*.

> A film is a **series** of images displayed at high speed.

*Sequence* is usually used for "a number of related actions or events that happen or come one after another," as in *a sequence of odd numbers*. A sequence usually has an order that follows some inner logic or relationship pattern.

> Film creates the illusion of movement by putting together a **sequence** of frames in which actions progress very slightly from one to the next.

CORPUS

**C.** Decide whether these things are or involve a series (*S*) or a sequence (*Q*). Use your dictionary to check the meanings of new words. Discuss your decisions with a partner. Think of one more series and sequence.

___ 1. issues of a monthly magazine     ___ 4. a soap opera

___ 2. events leading up to a discovery     ___ 5. Spider-Man™ comic books

___ 3. operating a camera     ___ 6. driving from one place to another

Series: _____

Sequence: _____

What is the difference between *transit* and *transition*?

*Transit* is usually used to refer to "the act of moving or being taken from one place to another." Some common terms are *mass transit* and *rapid transit*, which refer to forms of transportation that carry people.

> *Edgerton produced dramatic still photographs of fast-moving objects in **transit**, such as bullets in flight.*

*Transition* is generally used more to talk about "the process of changing from one condition or form to another."

> *StroMotion™ allows viewers to fully appreciate the technique and the quality of aerial maneuvers and highlights the different phases and their **transitions**.*

A person or thing in *transit* is moving or traveling from one place to another.

A person or thing in *transition* is changing form or nature in some way.

**D.** **What types of transitions might these things go through? Discuss your ideas in a small group.**

1. a caterpillar
2. a teenager
3. a small business
4. an ambitious worker
5. a senior citizen
6. a story someone thinks of

## Vocabulary Activities  STEP II: Sentence Level

*Hence* has two common functions. Sometimes it is a logical transition word, meaning "as a result."

> *These dolls were handmade; **hence**, they are expensive.*

It can also mean "from now" or "in the future," though this usage is becoming somewhat formal and old-fashioned.

> *Today everyone is excited about fashion trends that will be boring and out of style a year **hence.***

**E.** Complete these sentences using the word *hence*.

1. He ate a lot of sweet, fatty foods and never exercised; hence,

   *he gained a lot of weight.* .

2. The team's star player was injured the day before the big game; hence,

   _____ .

3. When she was young she was stung by a bee; hence,

   _____ .

4. Both of his parents were musicians; hence,

   _____ .

5. A = B and B = C; hence,

   _____ .

Before digital photography was invented, photographers had to allow film to be struck by light—they had to *expose* film—in order to capture an image.

> After first **exposing** the film, photographers used a series of chemicals to develop the image.

More generally, *expose* means to show something or make something visible. Usually this is something hidden, concealed, or previously unknown.

> The bright lights **exposed** all the cracks and lines on the wall.

Note: *Expose* and *display* are both synonyms of *show*, but *display* is generally used to talk about showing things to make them look good, possibly to sell something or attract attention. *Expose* is often used to show something shameful, corrupt, immoral, or dishonest that had been hidden or disguised.

C CORPUS

**F.** In your notebook, rewrite these sentences using the cues in parentheses. Check your dictionary for help with new words and meanings. Be prepared to read aloud or discuss your sentences in class.

___ 1. The heavy rains have eroded the riverbank. Now all the roots of the trees and bushes are bare. (*expose*)

   *The heavy rains have washed away the riverbank and exposed the tree roots.*

___ 2. Before coming to the city for school, she had never had the opportunity to appreciate the arts. (*exposure*)

___ 3. The businessman had to resign after the newspaper found out about his questionable financial deals and published the information. (*exposé*)

___ 4. Parents sometimes allow their children to catch a contagious disease, like measles or chicken pox, so that the children will be immune to the disease as adults. (*be exposed to*)

___ 5. The hikers who got lost in the mountains died because they were out in severe weather for too long. (*exposure*)

___ 6. Be sure to put sunscreen on any uncovered areas so that your skin doesn't burn. (*exposed*)

___ 7. At a home design show, you can get great ideas for decorating your apartment. (*exposition* or *expo*)

___ 8. His clients found out he was a fraud and told the police about how he sold them nonexistent property. (*exposed as a fraud*)

**G.** Read the sentences in activity F again and decide whether each exposure is positive (P) or negative (N). Discuss your reasoning in a small group.

**H.** Self-Assessment Review: Go back to page 65 and reassess your knowledge of the target vocabulary. How has your understanding of the words changed? What words do you feel most comfortable with now?

## Writing and Discussion Topics

**Write about or discuss the following topics.**

1. Photography has expanded human perception in various new ways. What new views of the universe, our planet, or nature have become available to us through photography? How have these views influenced the way we think about things?

2. Is photography a science, an art form, or both? Support your answer with one or more example photographs.

3. Imagine what it would be like if we saw everything in StroMotion™. What kind of advantage might it provide? What kind of disadvantage might result?

# The Physics of Fun

## In this unit, you will

> read about the engineering behind the development of amusement park rides.

> review skimming and making predictions.

> increase your understanding of the target academic words for this unit.

**READING SKILL** Making Inferences

## Self-Assessment

Think about how well you know each target word, and check (✓) the appropriate column. I have…

| TARGET WORDS | never seen the word before | seen the word but am not sure what it means | seen the word and understand what it means | used the word, but am not sure if correctly | used the word confidently in *either* speaking *or* writing | used the word confidently in *both* speaking *and* writing |
|---|---|---|---|---|---|---|
| **AWL** | | | | | | |
| 🔑 adult | | | | | | |
| automate | | | | | | |
| 🔑 brief | | | | | | |
| 🔑 credit | | | | | | |
| distort | | | | | | |
| 🔑 draft | | | | | | |
| input | | | | | | |
| 🔑 obtain | | | | | | |
| paragraph | | | | | | |
| 🔑 prior | | | | | | |
| regulate | | | | | | |
| 🔑 revise | | | | | | |
| 🔑 tradition | | | | | | |
| violate | | | | | | |

🔑 Oxford 3000™ keywords

**Outside the Reading** What do you know about amusement parks? Watch the video on the student website to find out more.

## Before You Read

Read these questions. Discuss your answers in a small group.

1. Are you afraid of heights, or do you enjoy being up high? What is one experience you've had with visiting a high place?

2. What is your favorite amusement park ride? Describe why you like it and how it makes you feel.

3. What are some things that engineers need to think about when they build something that will hold people?

**REVIEW A SKILL** **Skimming and Making Predictions** (See p. 34)

Skim the article and make a prediction to answer the question. When you finish reading, check your prediction to see if it was correct. What is the main idea of this article?

## Read

The following article from a popular science magazine tells the story of the first amusement ride.

# A Whale of a Wheel

In 1889, France hosted the first *Exposition Universelle*, or World's Fair, in Paris. In every way, the Exposition was so big, so glamorous, so exotic that no one believed
5 anything could ever surpass it. The city of Chicago, Illinois, decided to try.

The Chicago World's Fair was held in 1893, but planning and building started much sooner. The Fair's organizers wanted to show the
10 world that the United States, and specifically Chicago, was just as capable of grand artistic and technological wonders as France. The centerpiece of the Paris Exposition was an elegant tower of steel tapering up to the sky. It was
15 designed by Gustav Eiffel and gave daring visitors a view of Paris that took their breath away. The organizers of the Chicago World's Fair had to come up with something even more magnificent.

The Ferris wheel at the Chicago World's Fair

Finding a suitable design to rival the Eiffel
20 Tower proved difficult. Architect Daniel H. Burnham was in charge of the project for the Chicago World's Fair. He received dozens of proposals from engineers and architects around the country to build various kinds of towers.
25 One day, he received a **brief** proposal and rough **draft** of plans for something more unbelievable

and outrageous than any **prior** proposal. The author of this proposal was George Washington Gale Ferris Jr.

30  Ferris proposed building a gigantic wheel that people could ride on as it turned. Burnham rejected Ferris's proposal. He could not believe that such a thing could be safe. It must **violate** the laws of physics. Its own weight would surely
35  **distort** the metal beams, causing it to turn irregularly and eventually collapse. Despite Burnham's fears, Ferris knew his design was sound. He knew that equal pressure applied to every spot on the wheel would balance the
40  forces acting on it. Physics was on his side.

Ferris **revised** the proposal three times and drew up many more **drafts** of engineering plans. He added countless **paragraphs** of detailed explanation on the engineering
45  required. He got other engineers to inspect his plans and confirm their soundness. Ferris finally **obtained** Burnham's approval in December 1892 and began construction immediately. Soon the wheel towered over the city. By opening day in
50  May 1893, the Ferris wheel was already the star of the Chicago World's Fair.

Robert Graves was a reporter for the newspaper, *The Alleghenian*. He visited the World's Fair and described the Ferris wheel
55  for readers:

What is the principle, the chief principle, on which the wheel is constructed? It is that of a bicycle wheel…. The lower half of the wheel simply hangs from the mighty axle
60  [center bar], and this lower half supports the upper half by means of the steel framework of its two rims [sides]…. The wheel, though apparently rigid in its construction, has just enough elasticity to make this method of
65  support possible, and yet not enough elasticity to produce any appreciable trembling or slipping effect.

The wheel was supported by two 140-foot (43-meter) steel towers. The 45-foot (14-meter)
70  axle was the largest single piece of forged steel at the time in the world. The wheel itself had a diameter of 250 feet (72 meters), a circumference of 825 feet (251 meters), and a maximum height of 264 feet (80 meters). Between the two rims of
75  the wheel, Ferris hung 36 wooden carriages, like railroad cars, that could hold 60 people each.

Every car hung from its own axle. This meant that the cars would swing slightly back and forth as the wheel slowly rotated, but they, and the
80  people inside them, always stayed upright.

The Ferris wheel turned by the power of steam. Two huge boilers, located off the main fairgrounds, generated steam and kept it under high pressure. A system of underground pipes
85  delivered the high-pressure steam to a large wheel on the ground under the Ferris wheel. The energy **input** from the steam caused the ground wheel to rotate, which drove the movement of the whole structure.

90  The ground wheel and the axle of the Ferris wheel were connected to each other by a massive chain that wrapped around them both. The ground wheel and the axle both had a band of raised pieces around them, called sprockets.
95  The links of the chain fit over the sprockets and held the chain in place. As the steam from the boilers forced the ground wheel to rotate, the chain was pulled along the sprockets. This caused the axle above to rotate as well. The axle
100  then turned the Ferris wheel. A series of brakes and other control devices **regulated** the energy **input** to keep the wheel's movement smooth and steady.

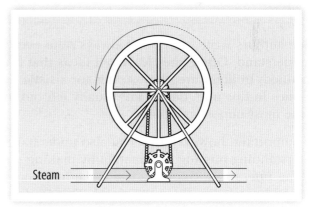

Steam forced the ground wheel to rotate, causing the Ferris wheel to turn.

Ferris was given **credit** for the success of the
105  Chicago World's Fair. His wheel was not only a technological marvel, but a thing of beauty. In fact, the fair's organizers worried that Ferris might have done his job too well. The Ferris wheel seemed too light, too delicate to support
110  itself. History records, however, that well over a million passengers rode the wheel during the Fair without incident.

The influence of Ferris's engineering and entertainment marvel is still clear today. In 1999,
115  London, England, continued the **tradition** of marking momentous occasions by erecting a Ferris wheel. The London Eye, the largest Ferris wheel in the world, was built to celebrate the beginning of the new millennium. On a smaller
120  scale, Ferris wheels of various sizes and types are attractions at fairs and amusement parks around the world. More than a century after it first dazzled visitors at the Chicago World's Fair, the Ferris wheel still has the power to fascinate,
125  thrill, and amaze. ■

## Reading Comprehension

Mark each sentence as *T* (true) or *F* (false) according to the information in Reading 1.

___ 1. The 1889 World's Fair in Paris hosted the first Ferris wheel.

___ 2. Daniel Burnham first rejected plans for the Ferris wheel because he thought it was unsafe.

___ 3. People in the Ferris wheel stayed upright as the wheel turned because the carriages they sat in were locked into place and did not move.

___ 4. A giant chain forced steam from the boilers into the ground wheel, which in turn caused the sprockets to rotate the axle. The axle then turned the Ferris wheel.

___ 5. Ferris wheels continue to be popular tourist attractions, as evidenced by the construction of the London Eye, the largest Ferris wheel in the world.

## READING SKILL    Making Inferences

### LEARN

When authors write, they don't always state every idea that they want you to understand. Often, they leave out ideas that they think don't need to be explained. In literature, they do this for artistic reasons. In factual articles, like the ones in this unit, details are usually left out in order to keep the text focused on the most important points.

It is important, however, that you also understand the unstated ideas in a text. Understanding missing information by making guesses is called *inferring*, or making *inferences*. Good readers make inferences based on other ideas in the text and knowledge about the world. This leads to a fuller understanding of the author's ideas and intentions.

### APPLY

Infer the answers to these questions. Then, on the line below, cite evidence from Reading 1 and explain how it supports your inference.

1. Before the Chicago world's fair, what was the general opinion about Chicago?

   a. It was an amazing, exciting city.       c. It was a smelly, disgusting swamp.

   b. It was not as impressive as Paris.       d. It had a large, beautiful lake.

Evidence: *The Fair's organizers wanted to show that the United States, specifically Chicago, was just as capable of grand artistic and technological wonders as France. (If the organizers wanted to prove this, it must mean it was not accepted as fact.)*

2. How were passengers able to stay upright as the wheel rotated?

   a. Each car was attached to its own axle.

   b. The wheel was powered by steam.

   c. The wheel had a large diameter.

   d. The main axle was made of forged steel.

Evidence: _____

_____

_____

3. Why was Ferris's proposal considered outrageous?

   a. It was larger than the other proposals.

   b. It was more expensive than the other proposals.

   c. It seemed physically impossible to build.

   d. It was far more beautiful than the Eiffel Tower.

Evidence: _____

_____

_____

4. Why did Burnham eventually approve Ferris's proposal?

   a. He knew the wheel would be popular and attract tourists to the fair.

   b. The approval of other engineers helped convince him it would be safe.

   c. He didn't get any other proposals that interested him as much.

   d. He thought it would be more impressive than the Eiffel Tower.

Evidence: _____

_____

_____

5. Why was the Ferris wheel the star of the fair even before opening day?

   a. Because it was more beautiful than the Eiffel Tower in France

   b. Because it was a lot of fun to ride on a wheel above the city

   c. Because the mechanics of its design were interesting to engineers

   d. Because people could see it being built and got excited about it

Evidence: _____

_____

_____

**A.** Read this passage about an activity that requires precision engineering. Fill in the blanks with the target vocabulary in the box.

| | | | |
|---|---|---|---|
| credit | obtain | regulations | revised |
| drafted | prior to | revise | violate |
| input | regulate | | |

Bungee jumping is a popular activity for the thrill-seeking type. It involves jumping from great heights with an elastic rope attached to your ankle. Just (1) _____ the moment when you would hit the ground, the elastic rope snaps you back up into the air.

Originally, a form of bungee jumping was practiced by people living on a few islands in the South Pacific. Modern bungee jumpers have (2) _____ the materials and methods of the sport and transformed it into a huge commercial enterprise around the world.

Bungee jumping businesses employ people with a strong knowledge of engineering to (3) _____ data on many different aspects of the activity: the distance of the drop, the elasticity of the ropes, the effects of factors such as weather conditions and a person's weight and height. These engineers seek the (4) _____ of other experts, and even the bungee jumpers themselves, to help them create safe conditions.

Because of the danger involved in the sport and the complicated nature of the calculations involved, some places have (5) _____ legislation to (6) _____ the bungee jumping industry. These lawmakers deserve (7) _____ for improving safety standards. The bungee jumping industry welcomes these (8) _____ , since they clarify the steps they need to take to improve safety. Companies that (9) _____ the regulations can be sued by injured customers. Most places continue to (10) _____ their laws as they learn more about the physics of bungee jumping.

**B.** What is your opinion? Circle the answer that best reflects what you think. Discuss your answers with a partner.

1. Which of these is the *briefest* activity for people your age?

   a. Eating lunch on a school or work day

   b. Getting ready for the day in the morning

   c. Having a phone conversation with their mother or father

2. Which of these is the worst thing to *violate*?

   a. A company or school policy

   b. An agreement with a friend

   c. The trust of a family member

3. Which of these is the most difficult thing to *draft*?

   a. Plans to build a house

   b. A chapter for a book

   c. A piece of legislation

4. Which of these things is the most difficult to *obtain*?

   a. A high-paying job

   b. An advanced degree

   c. Power over others

5. Which of these actions can most improve a *paragraph*?

   a. Revising it

   b. Rewriting it completely

   c. Leaving it alone

**C.** Put a check (✓) next to the activities that you think should be regulated by the government. Then, in a small group, choose the five that are most important to regulate and rank them, with *1* as the most important and *5* as the least important. Share your answers with the class.

___ selling cigarettes

___ owning pets

___ wearing seatbelts in a car

___ having children

___ wearing a bicycle helmet

___ owning a gun

___ place of residence

___ daily water use

___ eating unhealthy foods

___ violent movies

**D.** Choose the best collocation (words that go together) in parentheses to complete the sentence. Write the complete sentences in your notebook. Compare sentences with a partner.

1. Information (*obtained by / obtained with / obtained against / obtained for*) child safety researchers indicates that many playground designs are unsafe for children.

2. Playgrounds are (*credited for / credited in / credited with / credited to*) causing over 150,000 accidents each year, most of which are due to design flaws like inappropriately high structures or unnecessarily hard surfaces.

3. These poorly designed playgrounds exist partly because few places have drafted (*regulations on / regulations against / regulations with / regulations from*) playground safety.

4. The government tries to ensure that school playgrounds do not violate any of the engineering standards set for child safety, but it does not give (*input in / input from / input on / input for*) public parks.

5. As parents become more concerned about outdoor play equipment that they purchase for their children, some companies have begun to cover their packaging with (*paragraphs at / paragraphs from / paragraphs of / paragraphs to*) explanation about the safety standards they use to design their products, or, at the very least, a brief list of its safety features.

**E.** Read these sentences about another kind of entertainment that uses physics for fun. Then rephrase the sentences in your notebook using the target vocabulary in parentheses. There may be several possible answers. Compare sentences with a partner.

A Canopy Tour

1. A Canopy Tour is an activity in which people travel in short sliding jumps on a system of cables and platforms through the tops of the trees in a rainforest. (*brief*)

   *A Canopy Tour is an activity in which people travel in brief sliding jumps on a system of cables and platforms through the tops of the trees in a rainforest.*

2. It is not descended from a local ancient cultural ritual, but originated in Central America in the 1970s, when it was developed by scientists to research local plants and wildlife that were previously inaccessible. (*tradition, prior*)

3. As Canopy Tours have developed into tourist attractions in a variety of tropical locales, many businesses have received permission to operate them. (*obtained*)

4. As the tours increase in popularity, different countries have developed a variety of rules for safety—some stricter than others—and the Association for Challenge Course Technology helps inform consumers about which tour programs break these rules. (*regulations, violate*)

5. In addition, groups of tour providers have written voluntary guidelines with sections detailing regulations for guide training, equipment standards, and safety inspections. (*drafted, paragraphs*)

To *distort* means "to change the shape or sound of something." *Distortion* is the result.

*The old mirror is not flat, so it **distorts** my reflection and makes me look very tall.*

It is often used in a more figurative way, to mean "misrepresent."

*Many people felt the senator **distorted** the facts in order to sway public opinion in his favor.*

CORPUS

**F.** Reword these sentences in your notebook using a form of *distort*. Compare your sentences with a partner.

1. When cartographers make maps, they have to change the shape of countries and oceans in order to make a three-dimensional object fit in two dimensions.

   *When cartographers make maps, they have to distort the shape of countries and oceans in order to represent a three-dimensional planet in two dimensions.*

2. With maps that use the Mercator Projection, the north-south and east-west angles have the same amount of stretching, which makes land masses far from the equator appear unusually large.

3. Although use of the Mercator Projection has been criticized as causing the production of inaccurate shapes, it has been used for many years and is still very popular.

4. Recently, developers in Dubai used the Mercator Projection to change the shape of the coastline, creating "The World," a group of man-made islands that look like land masses on a map of the world.

5. Islands representing different countries can be bought by private owners, who can then further change their shapes, creating tourist attractions and amusements.

## Before You Read

Read these questions. Discuss your answers in a small group.

1. Have you ever been on a roller coaster? If so, what was that experience like? If not, why not? Would you like to ride on one?

2. Do you think most amusement park rides are safe? Why or why not?

3. What effect do roller coasters and other rides have on the body? How are these effects different from the normal stresses people experience every day?

## Read

This magazine article discusses the physics of safety related to the engineering of thrill rides.

# SUMMER FUN UNDER SCRUTINY

When summer hits, it's amusement park season. Crowds rush the open doors of theme parks across the world. In Istanbul, it's Luna Park. Paris, Tokyo,
5 and Los Angeles have Disneyland. Some people wait in line for hours for their favorite rides. Roller coasters provide much of the draw for young and old alike. There's the thrill of the height, the rush of sound, the feeling of being
10 weightless, and then the falling down, down, down! In fact, the names of the rides alone hint at the thrill that is to come: Australia has the Tower of Terror and Japan the Steel Dragon.

But is this summertime **tradition** safe? A quick
15 glance at the national newspaper headlines from July 2011 makes the thrills seem hardly worth the risk. "Freak roller coaster accidents cause concern over their safety," reads one article. At a theme park in New York in the United States, a
20 twenty-nine-year-old father was thrown from the roller coaster Ride of Steel as it made its rapid descent. He was wearing a safety belt at the time. A couple of days later in the state of Texas,
riders were suspended 14 stories up in the air
25 for over 30 minutes before being able to climb down an emergency stairway to safety.

These accidents lead to questions about how roller coasters are **regulated.** What went wrong on the Ride of Steel to result in a man's
30 death? Many times in accidents such as these, the cause is not clear. In this particular case, an investigation by the Department of Labor was conducted to **obtain** more information. The department found that it was
35 not that the roller coaster was unsafe, but that the ride operators **violated** the rules. On this ride, safety devices restrain the legs, shins, and lap to secure each person in the car. The rules required riders to have both legs so they
40 can be properly secured on the ride. The man who was thrown, however, didn't have either of his legs, but he was still permitted to board the ride.

As a result of this death, the park
45 implemented new practices. Now all employees who operate the ride must be

retrained in safety procedures, new signs must be posted that specify the safety regulations, and park management must now review the safety
50 procedures **prior** to a ride operator's shift.

However, it's not just the adventure seekers that are in danger. Rides aren't fully **automated**; they need operators. Unfortunately, operators have also been the victims of accidents. A twenty-four-
55 year-old ride operator in Sautron, France, died when he left the control booth and his legs were crushed under the ride. In order for rides to operate safely, both riders and operators have to adhere to rules and restrictions. In the Ride of
60 Steel accident, the theme park was initially accused of employing ride operators that were under the legal **adult** age of eighteen. New York state law requires ride operators to be at least eighteen years old. In later reports, the park was
65 able to clarify that the operators of the ride were over eighteen.

Even if passengers and ride operators follow guidelines, are roller coasters safe? Each year, as amusement parks compete to draw in crowds,
70 new, faster, and taller roller coasters are built. In 2011, Japan opened what is claimed to be the world's steepest roller coaster. Its name *Takibisha* means "high-flying car." And in fact, riders may feel like they are flying or actually falling as they
75 experience its steepest drop from the dizzying height of 141 feet at an angle of 121 degrees. In Abu Dhabi, the roller coaster Formula Rossa holds the record for the fastest speed at 149 miles per hour. If this sounds fast, that's because it is. The
80 average passenger airplane, such as a Boeing 757, reaches a speed of about 160 to 180 miles per hour at takeoff.

In fact, the same software and technology being used to develop aircraft like Boeing's is what is
85 making such dramatic heights, speeds, curves, and thrills possible on new roller coasters. Jim Seay, president of the roller coaster design firm Premier Rides, explains in an article for *Popular Mechanics* that roller coasters are able to reach
90 extreme speeds and heights because of "new engineering tools, quicker computers and exotic materials." He adds that "high-tech materials like carbon-fiber composites opened the door to more sophisticated designs because they reduce

People of all ages love the thrill of roller coasters.

95 weight and the resulting stresses on large support structures." This new technology affects everything from the shape and design of the roller coaster to the motors that power it. For example, computer-aided design allows
100 engineering feats resulting in rides like Fahrenheit, in Pennsylvania, that propels riders down at a 97-degree angle. That is seven degrees past a vertical drop. New linear induction motors, which are designed to
105 accelerate an object to a very high speed with magnetic waves, are used in a ride at Six Flags in the United States. Riders reach speeds of 70 miles per hour in only 4 seconds.

It's no wonder that critics and safety
110 advocates worry about the trauma caused by traveling at such speeds. Douglas Smith, a University of Pennsylvania neurologist, conducted tests in 2003 to analyze how a person's head rotates while on a ride. It's the
115 rotation of the head, along with the excessive speeding up and slowing down, that is the main cause of brain injury. He found that people's head rotation and acceleration and deceleration while on rides were not at levels
120 that would cause brain injury. Since then, he's repeated the study, and initial data support his first findings.

Yet doctors will continue to issue warnings, as will riders who have experienced injury
125 firsthand. A recent article in *Popular Mechanics* links roller coaster riding with

hearing loss. One doctor, whose patient turned his head during a ride and suffered an eardrum-blasting pressure, explained: "The faster the ride
130 moves and the larger the change in altitude, the higher the force that is applied to the ear." This is why he now recommends that people look straight ahead while riding roller coasters. However, Bryan Pfister, a biomedical engineer at New Jersey's
135 Science and Technology University, conducted a study that found the effect on the head during a roller coaster ride to be similar to the wallops one receives while pillow-fighting or playing sports.

With his findings, he questions whether the
140 accidents from roller coasters are a real threat or a freak occurrence.

It's no question that accidents from roller coasters can be serious and even fatal, and that the public and the amusement parks
145 themselves can benefit from a serious look at ride regulations and requirements. The future is only going to bring more innovative design and more pulse-pumping rides. And for every new roller coaster, there's likely to be a line of
150 eager riders wrapping around the corner.

## Reading Comprehension

Mark each sentence as *T* (true) or *F* (false) according to the information in Reading 2.

___ 1. The world's fastest roller coaster moves at higher speeds than a Boeing jet.

___ 2. New York State Law requires that ride operators be at least sixteen years of age.

___ 3. According to Douglas Smith's 2003 findings, ride acceleration and deceleration were not at levels that would cause brain injury.

___ 4. Abu Dhabi's Formula Rossa is the steepest roller coaster in the world.

___ 5. An investigation into the accident that occurred on the Ride of Steel revealed that ride operators had not followed safety regulations.

## READING SKILL   Making Inferences

### APPLY

Answer these questions in your notebook. You will need to make inferences. Support your inferences with evidence from Reading 2. Discuss your answers and inferences with a partner.

1. How does Pfister's study support the argument that roller coasters do not cause brain injury?

2. What can be inferred from the following sentence?

   *Each year, as amusement parks compete to draw in crowds, new, faster, and taller roller coasters are built.*

3. Are the New York regulations for ride operators necessary? Why or why not?

**A.** Read these excerpts from an article about New Jersey state's (in the United States) safety regulations on amusement parks. For each excerpt, cross out the one word or phrase in parentheses with a different meaning from the other three choices. Use a dictionary to help you understand new words. Compare your answers with a partner.

1. According to New Jersey's plan, forces on a new ride must not exceed limits outlined by the state. New rides that exceed those limits are not (*clearly / immediately / instantly / automatically*) rejected, but will be subject to a more extensive review.

2. The plan is based partly on research done in Russia. Legislators there have (*written / accepted / drafted / composed*) a set of (*regulations / rules / structures / policies*) based on military aviation tests on physically healthy (*adult / grown / mature / serious*) individuals.

3. New Jersey regulators also looked at research done in Europe on neck injuries, although this research studied only the (*usual / traditional / dangerous / conventional*) gravity-driven coasters, not the newer, potentially more dangerous coasters.

4. New Jersey regulators relied on research from other countries because they were unable to (*review / acquire / obtain / get*) injury records for the 150 U.S. roller coasters that they studied.

**B.** Which of these tasks have been automated? Discuss your answers with a partner.

___ washing dishes

___ brushing your teeth

___ watering the garden

___ answering the phone

___ making coffee

___ washing clothes

___ cleaning the floor

___ mending torn clothes

___ feeding a child

___ brushing your hair

**C.** Most societies regulate certain activities that can be done only by adults. Some also have activities that can only be done by children. Next to each item below, write—

> A for activities regulated for adults
>
> C for activities regulated for children
>
> B if an activity is regulated for both adults and children
>
> N if no regulation exists.

| | |
|---|---|
| ___ earn money for working | ___ get a secondary school degree |
| ___ stay at home alone | ___ open a bank account |
| ___ ride the bus alone | ___ have an email address |
| ___ drive a car | ___ watch a violent movie |
| ___ get married | ___ play on a sports team |
| ___ buy cigarettes | |

Compare answers with a partner. Discuss how each item is regulated, who is responsible for the regulation, and how regulation changes in different contexts.

**D.** Complete the passage using the target vocabulary in the box.

| | | | |
|---|---|---|---|
| brief | input | prior to | violated |
| credit | paragraph | revise | |

Many amusement parks ask for (1) _____ from lawyers when creating their safety policies. They want to protect guests from danger, but they also want to prevent injured customers from taking them to court. For example, while waiting in line, park visitors may see a sign posted near the entrance with a lengthy (2) _____ explaining who should or should not go on this ride. Guests may also have to watch a (3) _____ safety demonstration (4) _____ getting on the ride. Then, if riders are injured, the park cannot be held responsible for the injury. The park can show that the visitors knew the safety policies but (5) _____ them anyway.

A lawsuit from an injured rider can damage the reputation of an amusement park for years. Legal advisers carefully (6) _____ the warnings on a regular basis to make sure they are up to date and cover every possible problem. Park owners (7) _____ their strict safety policies and the help of their legal advisers with protecting their good name and their profits.

**E.** Most countries have regulations that describe how people should behave when they drive cars. In the boxes on the left, write examples of driving regulations that you think are important. On the right, write examples of punishments that you think would be appropriate for people who violate those regulations.

| Driving Regulation | Penalty for Violation |
| --- | --- |
| No talking on the cell phone while driving | large fine |
|  |  |
|  |  |
|  |  |
|  |  |
|  |  |
|  |  |
|  |  |

**F.** Imagine that you have the chance to interview the inventor of one of the rides described in this unit. What would you ask? Write interview questions using as many of the target words in this unit as you can. You might have to do some research online. Consider these issues as you prepare your interview questions:

- how the ride works
- what it looks like
- why people like it
- the history of how the inventor developed this ride
- what sort of safety guidelines it requires

Be prepared to use your questions to role play an interview with a partner in class.

**G.** Think of a traditional game you are familiar with and that you think a visitor from another part of the world would find interesting. Write a brief description of it in the chart. Then, consider what safety regulations would be necessary for people taking part in it for the first time. Be prepared to present your ideas to the class or discuss them in a small group.

| Traditional Game | Regulations |
|---|---|
| Hopscotch—draw boxes on the ground with different numbers and throw a rock into one of the boxes. Then, hop on one leg in all the boxes, except the one with the rock. | 1. Do not throw the rock at other people.<br>2. Wear athletic shoes so you don't twist your ankle.<br>3. Draw the hopscotch boxes on soft mats so people who fall don't hurt themselves. |
| | |

**H.** Self-Assessment Review: Go back to page 81 and reassess your knowledge of the target vocabulary. How has your understanding of the words changed? What words do you feel most comfortable with now?

## Writing and Discussion Topics

Write about or discuss the following topics.

1. People participate in other thrill-seeking activities besides roller coasters and bungee jumping. Can you name some? Have you participated in these activities? Would you like to? Why do you think people are attracted to thrill seeking?

2. What would a roller coaster look like if a non-engineer designed it, for example, a scuba diver, or a small child, or a mouse? Choose any "designer" you want, and use your imagination.

3. What kinds of regulations have you encountered at amusement parks? Did you agree with the regulations or find them unnecessary? Why?

# UNIT 7

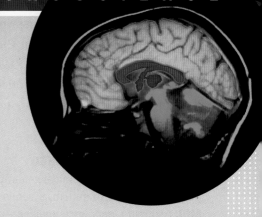

# Mind Wide Open

## In this unit, you will

> read about the latest developments in brain research.
> learn about how the brain perceives body sensations.
> increase your understanding of the target academic words for this unit.

**READING SKILL** Annotating and Highlighting a Text

## Self-Assessment
Think about how well you know each target word, and check (✓) the appropriate column. I have…

| TARGET WORDS | never seen the word before | seen the word but am not sure what it means | seen the word and understand what it means | used the word, but am not sure if correctly | used the word confidently in *either* speaking *or* writing | used the word confidently in *both* speaking *and* writing |
|---|---|---|---|---|---|---|
| **AWL** | | | | | | |
| 🔑 attach | | | | | | |
| 🔑 chapter | | | | | | |
| distinct | | | | | | |
| induce | | | | | | |
| 🔑 initial | | | | | | |
| insight | | | | | | |
| integrity | | | | | | |
| 🔑 internal | | | | | | |
| 🔑 minor | | | | | | |
| 🔑 obvious | | | | | | |
| scenario | | | | | | |
| sphere | | | | | | |
| trigger | | | | | | |
| visual | | | | | | |

🔑 Oxford 3000™ keywords

 **Outside the Reading** What do you know about neuroscience?
Watch the video on the student website to find out more.

## Before You Read

Read these questions. Discuss your answers in a small group.

1. Do you ever think about the way your mind works? How important is it to understand this in your everyday life? In your academic life?

2. Where do you think emotions come from? Are they physical or psychological?

3. What part of the mind or what mental process would you most hate to lose? Why?

**MORE WORDS YOU'LL NEED**

**adrenaline:** a bodily chemical generated in response to stress
**autistic:** referring to autism, which is a neurological disorder
**MRI:** magnetic resonance imaging—a medical imaging method using magnets
**paranormal:** not scientifically explainable

## READING SKILL    Annotating and Highlighting a Text

### LEARN

*Annotating*—making notes about what you read—will help you understand and remember the material. It will also make it easier to access the information if you need it in the future.

### APPLY

One form of annotation is **highlighting**. You can highlight by underlining parts of the text or by using a light colored marker to mark the text. To highlight, mark only these things as you read:

- main ideas
- key details
- interesting examples
- frequently mentioned people or places
- important dates or locations
- something strange or surprising
- anything you have a question about or disagree with

In the margins of the book—the blank spaces to the left and right of the text—**take notes** or make comments about why you highlighted the things you did. If necessary, use arrows to connect your notes with the highlighted lines.

As you read the texts in this unit, highlight them and take notes in the margins. Lines have been provided to help you.

🔊 **Read**

Read this *New York Times* book review of *Mind Wide Open*, by Steven Johnson.
In this book, Johnson gets to know his own mind a little better by using the tools
of modern neuroscience.

# Mind Wide Open
## by Jonathan Weiner

*MIND WIDE OPEN: Your Brain and the Neuroscience of Everyday Life*
by Steven Johnson

Until recently, people couldn't look into themselves directly to
explore what Gerard Manley Hopkins called our "inscapes."[1]
But now we can. With MRIs, PET scans, and many other
high-tech mirrors, we can see right through our own foreheads and
5   begin to watch our mental apparatus[2] in action.

The **scenario** for Steven Johnson's *Mind Wide Open* is this:
Johnson makes himself his own test subject to see what the
neuroscientists can show us about our attention spans, talents, moods,
thoughts, and drives—our *selves*. He got the idea for this voyage of
10   self-discovery a few years ago while he was hooked up to a
biofeedback[3] machine. Lying on a couch with sensors[4] **attached** to his
palms, fingertips, and forehead made him feel nervous, and he started
making jokes about it to the biofeedback guy. The machine was
designed to monitor adrenaline levels, like a lie detector machine. With
15   each joke he made, the monitor displayed a huge spike of adrenaline:
"I found myself wondering how many of these little chemical
subroutines are running in my brain on any given day? At any given
moment? And what would it tell me about myself if I could see them,
the way I could see those adrenaline spikes on the printout?"

20   Johnson writes the monthly Emerging Technology column for
*Discover* magazine, and is a contributing editor at *Wired*. He knows
how to make complicated science clear and easy to follow, and his style
is cheerful, honest, friendly—and filled with those nervous jokes. In
his last book, "Emergence," he explored the ways in which the
25   complicated behavior of brains, software, cities, and ant heaps can
emerge from the vastly simpler behavior of their smallest working
parts—from collections of nerve cells, bits and bytes, citizens and
ants—to become the webs and **spheres** of efficient mass circuitry.[5]

---

[1] *"inscapes":* a word created from "interior" and "landscape" to describe one's mental functions
[2] *apparatus:* equipment, machinery
[3] *biofeedback:* a process that makes bodily processes perceptible to the senses
[4] *sensors:* devices that respond to a physical stimulus and transmit a corresponding
impulse, such as an electrode that picks up a heartbeat and displays it on a screen
[5] *mass circuitry:* the complete pathway that electronic circuits flow through

Here he writes about some of the ways that the behavior of what we like to call our *self* emerges moment by moment from all kinds of separate tools and workshops in the brain, which neuroscientists call *modules*.

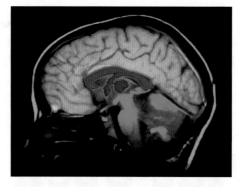

Johnson begins with a gift that most of us take for granted: mind reading. Even before we can talk, almost all of us know how to read subtle hints in the faces, voices, and gestures of the people around us. That is, we can do by instinct what neuroscientists are just learning to do with scanners and monitors.

To learn about his own mind-reading abilities, Johnson takes a famous test devised by the British psychologist Simon Baron-Cohen. In the test, you are shown a series of 36 different pairs of eyes on a computer screen. Each pair has a **distinctive** expression. For each, you have to choose one adjective from a set of four that Baron-Cohen provides: Is this pair of eyes despondent,[6] preoccupied, cautious, or regretful? Johnson finds that he has an instant gut reaction to each pair of eyes. But when he looks harder, he feels less and less sure what he sees.

Our natural ability to read people's faces is outside conscious thought. As with breathing or swallowing, we can't explain how we do it. Baron-Cohen and others believe that the skill depends partly on the *amygdala*, one of the brain's emotional centers. He has made brain scans of people taking his reading-the-eyes test using functional MRI, which reveals which parts of the brain are working hardest from moment to moment. When most people try to decode the emotion in a pair of eyes, their amygdalae light up. When autistic persons do it, their amygdalae are much dimmer.

In other **chapters**, Johnson explores some of the fear messages that are controlled by his amygdala: traumatic fears that were **triggered** by a near disaster when a storm blew in a big window in his apartment. He explores our brain chemistry, describing some of the natural "drugs" that we give ourselves without knowing it: adrenaline, oxytocin, serotonin, dopamine, cortisol. He learns how to recognize which natural high[7] he is riding, or which bad trip[8] he is enduring. He also learns some useful lessons about the ways our brains' drugs affect our memories. There's also a **chapter** about his sojourn in a $242-million MRI machine, in which he reads a passage by the Nobel Prize-winning neuroscientist Eric Kandel, and then reads a passage of his own. The test proves that nothing makes a writer's brain light up like reading his own words.

---

[6] *despondent:* very sad

[7] *high:* a feeling of great pleasure or happiness **induced** by natural chemicals or medications

[8] *trip:* an altered state of consciousness **induced** by natural chemicals or medications

Johnson's preoccupations, the weather systems of his own inner
75 life, keep cycling back **chapter** after **chapter**: his horror when that
window blew in and almost killed his wife; his moments of tenderness
gazing at their sleeping newborn son. As he explores his inner world
and the mental modules that help to shape it, we begin to feel that we
are right in there with him—and we have a new sense of what it means
80 to be human.

The best **chapter** is the last, when Johnson analyzes the current
view of the mind. It is **obvious** now that Sigmund Freud's most basic
**insight** was correct—there is more going on in there than we are
aware of. This is not new news, but Johnson brings it all alive. He
85 concludes: "Even the sanest among us have so many voices in our
heads, all of them competing for attention, that it's a miracle we ever
get anything done."

This is an entertaining and instructive ride inward to a place that
looks less familiar the better we get to know it. As Johnson says, "It's a
90 jungle in there."

"If a lion could talk we would not understand him," the
philosopher Ludwig Wittgenstein said. *Mind Wide Open* takes the point
closer to home. If every part of our brain could talk, we would not
understand ourselves. ■

## Reading Comprehension

Mark each sentence as *T* (true) or *F* (false) according to the information in Reading 1.
Look at your highlighting and notes to help you.

___ 1. Steven Johnson wrote *Mind Wide Open* to see what neuroscientists could
show us about the mind.

___ 2. Johnson used himself as a test subject.

___ 3. In his previous book, Johnson compared the complicated behavior of
brains, software, cities, and ants.

___ 4. Johnson believes that mind reading—the ability to interpret faces, voices,
and gestures—is a rare skill.

___ 5. The book reviewer criticizes Johnson for making simple science confusing
and hard to follow.

___ 6. Johnson believes that our ability to read people's faces is with us from birth.

___ 7. An MRI displays which parts of the brain are working hardest during a test.

___ 8. Johnson doesn't believe that the brain's control of the body's natural drugs
is important in dealing with fear or preserving memories.

**APPLY**

Write a one-paragraph summary in your notebook of the book review in Reading 1. Use your annotations and highlighting for reference. Answer these questions in your summary.

1. Is the book review positive or negative?
2. How does the mind-reading test work?

## Vocabulary Activities | STEP I: Word Level

**A.** Match the dictionary definitions for the word *attach* with the example sentences. Then answer the questions that follow. Discuss your answers with a partner.

| **Definitions** | **Sample sentences** |
|---|---|
| ___ 1. To fasten or connect one thing to another | a. Scientists attached no significance to the threat. |
| ___ 2. To think something or someone has a particular quality | b. She is attached to her family. |
| ___ 3. To feel a close connection with something or someone | c. Several files and some photos have been attached to this email. |
| ___ 4. To combine electronic files for the purpose of transmission | d. He attached the wires from the amplifier to the speakers. |

1. What have you recently attached to something else (not email)?
   *I recently attached a camera to my computer.*

2. What type of things do you send as email attachments?

3. What do you attach a lot of importance to?

4. What do you attach little or no importance to?

5. Who do you feel attached to?

6. What do you feel attached to?

**B.** Put each word in the box in the correct column, based on which target word it is a synonym for. Use your dictionary to check the meanings of new words. Compare your results with a partner.

| | | | |
|---|---|---|---|
| activate | cause | different | spark |
| add | clear | distinguishing | special |
| adhere | connect | fasten | start |
| apparent | conspicuous | plain | unique |

| obvious | trigger | attach | distinctive |
|---|---|---|---|
| _____ | _activate_ | _____ | _____ |
| _____ | _____ | _____ | _____ |
| _____ | _____ | _____ | _____ |
| _____ | _____ | _____ | _____ |

## Vocabulary Activities  STEP II: Sentence Level

The word *obvious* means "easily seen or understood." In essay writing, *obvious* and *obviously* can help you avoid longer phrases like "everyone knows" or "it's easy to see," and they can give your ideas an attitude of formality and authority.

> **Obviously**, the Internet has aided globalization.
>
> It is **obvious** that the Internet has aided globalization.

CORPUS

**C.** Complete the statements. Refer to Reading 1 for information. Compare your work with a partner.

1. Obviously, the human mind is _complex and mysterious._ _____

    _____

2. It is obvious that modern technology _____

    _____

3. It is obvious that author Steven Johnson is _____

    _____

4. Obviously, the book critic is recommending *Mind Wide Open* because

    _____

    _____

The word *insight* refers to someone's or something's understanding of the true nature of another person or thing. It usually takes the preposition *into*.

*The math teacher at their middle school has great **insight** <u>into</u> teenagers. She can always figure out how to get them to do their work and perform well.*

Insight can be given (or can attempt to be given) to others. Books, in particular, are often described as having or giving insight.

*The book gives a good **insight** <u>into</u> the lives of the poor in early 19th-century Europe.*

In other words, the book's author has explained his insight on this subject well. People who read the book are likely to come away with a greater understanding of the topic.

CORPUS

**D.** **Write questions about insight using the cues provided. Answer the questions in complete sentences. Then discuss your answers in a small group.**

1. parents / children

   *What insights might parents have into their children?*

   *Parents have insight into their children's likes and dislikes. They know, for example, what foods their kids will probably like, based on other things they like.*

2. book about psychology / unhappiness

   _____

   _____

   _____

3. best friends / each other

   _____

   _____

   _____

4. veterinarian / animal behavior

   _____

   _____

   _____

5. babysitter / family problems

   _____

   _____

   _____

6. anthropologist / workplace politics

   _____

   _____

   _____

## Before You Read

**Answer these questions. Discuss your answers in a small group.**

1. Have you ever had a strange experience that you could not explain? For example, did you ever sense that someone was watching you? What did you feel at the time? How did you feel later?

2. Did you or someone you know ever have an out-of-body experience (where you felt that you had left your body and then returned to it)? What was it like?

3. If you could leave your body and then return to it, would you do it? Why or why not? What might you learn from this experience?

## ◀)) Read

This *New York Times* article questions whether unexplained experiences might, in fact, have an explanation.

# Out-of-Body Experience? Your Brain Is to Blame

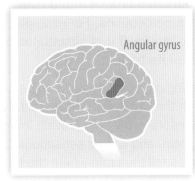

Angular gyrus

They are eerie[1] sensations, more common than one might think: A man describes the **distinct** feeling of a shadowy figure standing
5 behind him, and then turns around to find no one there. A woman feels herself leaving her body and floating in space, looking down on her physical body.

10 People often attribute such experiences to paranormal forces outside the **sphere** of material life. But according to recent work by neuroscientists, they can be **induced** by delivering mild electric current to specific spots in the brain.

15 In one woman, for example, a zap to a brain region—the angular gyrus—resulted in a sensation that she was hanging from the ceiling, looking down at her body. In another woman, electrical current delivered to the same area **triggered** a feeling that someone was behind her, intent on interfering with her actions.

20 The two women were being evaluated for epilepsy surgery at University Hospital in Geneva, Switzerland. Doctors implanted

---

[1] *eerie:* strange and frightening

electrodes into their brains to find the abnormal tissue causing
their seizures.[2] As each electrode was activated, stimulating a
different patch of brain tissue, the patient was asked to say what
25  she was experiencing.

Dr. Olaf Blanke, who carried out the procedures, is a neurologist
at the École Polytechnique Fédérale de Lausanne in Switzerland.
He said that the women had normal psychiatric histories and that
they were stunned by the bizarre nature of their experiences.

30  But this is not a film **scenario**, and there is nothing mystical
about these ghostly experiences, said Peter Brugger, a
neuroscientist at University Hospital in Zurich. Dr. Brugger is an
expert on phantom[3] limbs—the sensation of still feeling a limb
that has been amputated.

35  "The research shows that the self can be detached from the body
and can live a phantom existence on its own, as in an out-of-body
experience. It can also be felt outside of personal space, as in a
sense of a presence," Dr. Brugger said.

Scientists have gained new understanding of these odd bodily
40  sensations as they have learned more about how the brain works,
Dr. Blanke said. For example, researchers have discovered that
some areas of the brain combine information from several
senses. Vision, hearing, and touch are **initially** processed in the
primary sensory regions (eyes, ears, fingertips, etc). But then they
45  flow together, like smaller streams flowing into a river, to create
the wholeness of a person's perceptions. For example, a dog is
**visually** recognized far more quickly if it is simultaneously
accompanied by the sound of its bark.

These multisensory processing regions also build up perceptions of
50  the body as it moves through the world, Dr. Blanke said. Nerves in
the body act as sensors. Sensors in the skin provide information
about pressure, pain, heat, cold, and similar sensations. Sensors in
the joints, tendons, and bones tell the brain where the body is
positioned in space. Sensors in the ears track the sense of balance.
55  And sensors in the **internal** organs, including the heart, liver, and
intestines, provide an assessment of a person's emotional state.

Real-time information from the body, the space around the body, and
the subjective feelings from the body are also represented in
multisensory regions, Dr. Blanke said. And if these regions are directly
60  stimulated by an electric current, as in the cases of the two women he
studied, the **integrity** of the sense of body can be altered.

As an example, Dr. Blanke described the case of a 22-year-old
student who had electrodes implanted into the left hemisphere of
her brain in 2004.

---

[2] *seizures:* involuntary losses of control, sometimes accompanied by violent
movements associated with the condition of epilepsy
[3] *phantom:* thought of as real but actually not real

65 "We were checking language areas," Dr. Blanke said. The woman suddenly turned her head to the right. That made no sense, he said, because the electrode was nowhere near areas involved in the control of movement. Instead, the current was stimulating the angular gyrus, which blends vision with body sense.

70 Dr. Blanke applied the current again. Again, the woman turned her head to the right. "Why are you doing this?" he asked.

The woman replied that she had a weird sensation that another person was lying beneath her on the bed. The figure, she said, felt like a "shadow" that did not speak or move; it was young, more like 75 a man than a woman, and it wanted to interfere with her.

When Dr. Blanke turned off the current, the woman stopped looking to the right, and said the strange presence had gone away. Each time he reapplied the current, she once again turned her head to try to see the shadow figure.

80 When the woman sat up, leaned forward and hugged her knees, she said that she felt as if the shadow man was also sitting and that he was clasping her in his arms. She said it felt unpleasant. When she held a card in her right hand, she reported that the shadow figure tried to take it from her. "He doesn't want me to 85 read," she said.

Because the presence closely simulated the patient's body posture and position, Dr. Blanke concluded that the patient was experiencing an unusual perception of her own body, as a double. But for reasons that scientists have not been able to 90 explain, he said, she did not recognize that it was her own body she was sensing.

This impression of a mimicking, shadowy self-simulation can occur without electrical stimulation to the brain, Dr. Brugger said. It has been described by people who undergo sensory deprivation, as in 95 mountaineers trekking at high altitude or sailors crossing the ocean alone. It is also experienced by people who have suffered **minor** strokes or other disruptions in blood flow to the brain.

Six years ago, another of Dr. Blanke's patients underwent brain stimulation to the angular gyrus. The patient experienced a 100 complete out-of-body experience.

When the current flowed, she said: "I am at the ceiling. I am looking down at my legs."

When the current ceased, she said: "I'm back on the table now. What happened?"

105 Because the woman's felt position in space and her actual position in space did not match, her mind searched for the best way to turn her confusion into a coherent experience, Dr. Blanke said. She concluded that she must be floating up and away while looking downward.

110 Some schizophrenics[4], Dr. Blanke said, experience paranoid delusions[5] and the sense that someone is following them. They also sometimes confuse their own actions with the actions of other people. While the cause of these symptoms is not known, he said, multisensory processing areas may be involved.

115 When otherwise normal people experience bodily delusions, Dr. Blanke said, they are often completely confused. The felt sensation of the body is so real, so familiar, that people do not realize it is a creation of the brain.

Yet the sense of body **integrity** is rather easily tricked, Dr. Blanke
120 said. While it may be tempting to credit the supernatural when this body sense goes wrong, the true explanation is a very natural one. It is the brain's attempt to make sense of conflicting information. ■

---

[4] *schizophrenics:* people with schizophrenia, a mental disorder in which people confuse reality and imagination
[5] *paranoid delusions:* a mental condition that causes one to feel extreme jealously or a false belief that one is being harassed or is an extremely important person in the world

## Reading Comprehension

Mark each sentence as *T* (true) or *F* (false) according to the information in Reading 2. Use the dictionary to help you understand new words.

___ 1. Electrical stimulation of the brain can trigger out-of-body experiences.

___ 2. In the tests described, doctors implanted electrodes into the brains of psychologically disturbed and dysfunctional patients.

___ 3. The patients were able to describe their experiences as each electrode was activated.

___ 4. The patients were very surprised by their experiences in this procedure.

___ 5. Neuroscientists believe that out-of-body simulated doubles are actually ghosts with a mystical purpose.

___ 6. The feeling of being with a shadowy presence can only be induced by artificial electrical stimulation.

___ 7. Some areas of the brain combine information from several senses.

___ 8. A person's emotional state is reflected in the condition of internal organs, including the heart, liver, and intestines.

### APPLY

Write a one-paragraph summary of Reading 2 in your notebook. Use your annotations and highlighting for reference. Answer these questions in your summary.

1. Are out-of-body experiences generally perceived to be pleasant or unpleasant? Why?

2. How can the integrity, or wholeness, of a person's sense of themselves be altered?

3. How does Dr. Blanke explain out-of-body experiences?

## Vocabulary Activities    STEP I: Word Level

**A.** Complete the sentences about neuroscience pioneer Wilder Penfield using the target vocabulary in the box. Use each item one time. The synonyms in parentheses can help you.

| | | | |
|---|---|---|---|
| attached | distinctive | initial | minor |
| chapter | induce | insight | visual |

1. Canadian neuroscientist Wilder Penfield conducted the _____ (first) research into brain mapping in the 1920s and 30s.

2. Penfield discovered that gentle electrical stimulation of the brain could _____ (produce) the recall of images and sounds from a patient's memory.

3. Although Penfield was interested in mapping both _____ (seen) and auditory memories, he _____ (assigned) a lot of significance to the large number and variety of songs in patients' heads.

4. Each time Penfield applied the electrical stimulation, he asked the patient what he/she saw or heard—and thereby learned that each stimulated location held a _____ (particular) image, sound, or memory.

5. Penfield had the _____ (intelligence) to list and map many of the songs people had stored in their minds, from radio theme songs and musical show tunes to children's lullabies.

6. Penfield came to believe that the brain retained an almost perfect record of both major and _____ (unimportant) experiences from every _____ (period) of a person's life.

The word *sphere* can refer to any round object or something having a round dynamic, like this instance from Reading 1:

> "...brains, software, cities, and ant heaps ... become the webs and **spheres** of efficient mass circuitry."

In Reading 2, *sphere* refers to "an area of interest or activity":

> "People often attribute such experiences to paranormal forces outside the **sphere** of material life."

The related word *hemisphere* means "half of a sphere." In biology, it is used to refer to the left and right sides of the brain. In geography, it is used to refer to parts of the world.

> Most parts of the brain related to language are in the right **hemisphere**.

> In the northern **hemisphere**, winter is in December, January, and February.

C CORPUS

**B.** Categorize these synonyms for *sphere* by definition. (One of the words will be used twice.) Add any other synonyms for *sphere* you can think of to the lists.

| ball | domain | globe | zone |
|------|--------|-------|------|
| circle | field | planet | |

**round**

_____

_____

_____

_____

**area of interest or activity**

_____

_____

_____

_____

**C.** Complete these sentences using the words in the box. Compare answers with a partner.

| academic sphere | sphere of influence | wider sphere |
|-----------------|---------------------|--------------|
| hemispheres | spherical objects | |

1. Artists must be able to draw square, cylindrical, triangular, and _____ , like oranges and balls.

2. Historically, China has had a broad _____ in East Asia.

3. The globe can be divided into four _____ : Eastern, Western, Northern, and Southern.

4. The professor's work is little known outside the _____ of the university.

5. His books are detective stories, but he hopes that they will appeal to a _____ than only mystery lovers.

The adjective *minor* means "not very big, serious, or important, when compared to others." The noun form, *minority*, refers to the smaller number or part of a group.

> *A childhood disease resulted in her having a **minor** hearing loss.*

> *A small **minority** of the general population has epilepsy.*

The noun *minor* has two meanings. Academically, it means "a field of study chosen as a secondary area of academic specialization." (see Unit 2, *major*)

> *She is a biology major with a **minor** in economics.*

These concepts can also be expressed in verb form:

> *She is majoring in biology and **minoring** in economics.*

In law, a *minor* is any person who has not yet reached the legal age of an adult.

> *It is illegal to sell cigarettes to **minors**.*

**D.** **Give examples of these things. Discuss your answers with a partner.**

1. a minor problem: _a lightbulb that went out;_ _____
2. a minor injury: _____
3. a minor inconvenience: _____
4. a minority group: _____

## Vocabulary Activities   STEP II: Sentence Level

*Induce* has the meaning "to make or persuade someone to do something."

> *Nothing could **induce** him to change his mind.*

It can also mean "cause or produce."

> *The doctor gave her a drug that **induces** sleep.*

**E.** **What external or internal forces might induce these things? Discuss your answers in a small group. Choose the best three answers and share them with your classmates.**

1. laughter
2. sympathy
3. the telling of a secret
4. emigration from your country
5. hardship on a family
6. the loss of a person's mental integrity

A *scenario* is "one way that things may happen in the future."

People often try to predict possibilities by imagining the *worst-case scenario* and the *best-case scenario*.

> *The doctor said that the worst-case **scenario** is that the drugs don't work and her illness progresses quickly.*

**F.** Read these situations and discuss them with a partner. What is the worst-case scenario and best-case scenario for each? Discuss your ideas in a small group.

1. While driving home one night, you accidentally hit a parked car, causing minor damage. You accept responsibility and leave a note with your phone number.

2. This evening, you are going to meet your roommate's parents for the first time at a fancy, expensive restaurant.

3. You awake to realize that your alarm did not go off. You have slept through a very important test in your most difficult class.

4. Walking along the street toward your home, you get the distinct feeling that someone is following you.

**G.** Read the definitions and synonyms of *integrity*. Decide which meaning applies to each of the sample sentences. In most cases, more than one meaning may apply. Then rewrite the sentences in your notebook without using the target word.

a. following a strict moral code; honor; honesty

b. soundness; solidness, security, safety, stability

c. completeness, wholeness, unity

___ 1. After the earthquake, engineers inspected all campus buildings and found no signs of damage to their structural integrity.

___ 2. The integrity of the company's computer network may have been undermined by hackers.

___ 3. Academic integrity is essential for building trust between a student and teacher.

___ 4. The financial integrity of the business is based on its investments in a wide variety of related consumer products and on its commitment to customer service.

**H.** Self-Assessment Review: Go back to page 97 and reassess your knowledge of the target vocabulary. How has your understanding of the words changed? What words do you feel most comfortable with now?

## Writing and Discussion Topics

Write about or discuss the following topics.

1. Compare and contrast the way these work: a mind and a computer.

2. Compare and contrast the way these look and work: a mind and a city.

3. How might the human mind change in the future? What could induce these changes?

# Child Prodigies

## In this unit, you will

> read about child prodigies and the challenges they pose for their families and society.
> review making inferences.
> increase your understanding of the target academic words for this unit.

**READING SKILL** Recognizing Comparison and Contrast

## Self-Assessment

Think about how well you know each target word, and check (✓) the appropriate column. I have…

| TARGET WORDS | never seen the word before | seen the word but am not sure what it means | seen the word and understand what it means | used the word, but am not sure if correctly | used the word confidently in *either* speaking *or* writing | used the word confidently in *both* speaking *and* writing |
|---|---|---|---|---|---|---|
| **AWL** | | | | | | |
| 🔑 challenge | | | | | | |
| 🔑 concentrate | | | | | | |
| 🔑 considerable | | | | | | |
| 🔑 enormous | | | | | | |
| 🔑 environment | | | | | | |
| 🔑 expert | | | | | | |
| 🔑 factor | | | | | | |
| 🔑 focus | | | | | | |
| 🔑 intelligence | | | | | | |
| 🔑 normal | | | | | | |
| 🔑 pursue | | | | | | |
| 🔑 resource | | | | | | |
| 🔑 reveal | | | | | | |
| 🔑 technology | | | | | | |
| utilize | | | | | | |

🔑 Oxford 3000™ keywords

**Outside the Reading** What do you know about prodigies?
Watch the video on the student website to find out more.

## Before You Read

Read these questions. Discuss your answers in a small group.

1. Have you ever known anyone who was very, very smart? What could they do or what did they know that made them different from other people their age?

2. What can a family do to help or encourage a baby's mental development? Physical development? Emotional development?

3. Schools often want to know how intelligent children are. How do schools usually measure intelligence? What kinds of tools or tests do they use? What skills or abilities do they measure?

**MORE WORDS YOU'LL NEED**

**prodigy:** a person who is significantly advanced in a particular area; usually applied to children
**society:** the people of a particular culture who share general values and priorities

## Read

This magazine article spotlights the unusual abilities of some very special children.

# Child Prodigies

It seemed **normal** when Nguyen Ngoc Truong Son wanted to play chess with his parents. However, it was unusual when he **revealed** that he already knew how to play—
5 before anyone taught him. Apparently the two-year-old had learned all of the rules by watching his parents. After only one month of playing with them, he was winning all of the games. By age four, he was competing in
10 national tournaments. By age 12, he was Vietnam's youngest champion.

Another two-year-old child, Jay Greenberg, likewise surprised his parents by drawing pictures of musical instruments that he had never
15 seen. They soon discovered that Jay "heard music in his head." He began to compose music at age three. By age ten, he was attending the well-known Juilliard Conservatory in New York, composing full symphonies. Jay was noted not
20 only for the quality of his musical work, but also the speed at which he was able to produce it.

That is, while talented professional composers **normally** write five or six symphonies in a lifetime, Jay wrote five by the age of 12.

25 A third young child, Abigail Sin, was first introduced to piano lessons at age five and had what her tutor called an "unstoppable urge to master the keyboard." She became Singapore's most celebrated pianist by age ten.

30 Child prodigies such as these are a mystery to **experts** and non-**experts** alike. On the one hand, they attract praise and attention from everyone they meet; on the other hand, they attract criticism, and they find it difficult to fit in
35 with the rest of the world.

Child prodigies are highly **intelligent**, but this is not the only **factor** that sets them apart. They are considered prodigies because of their exceptional ability in one domain, or area.

40 **Experts** define *child prodigy* as "a young child who displays mastery of a field that is usually undertaken by adults." Child prodigies usually have abilities in structured areas such as language, math, drawing, chess, and music. They

45 are not as likely to appear in less structured domains such as medicine, law, or creative writing, areas that require experience.

Child prodigies can **focus** their attention for long periods of time, **concentrating** on tasks that

50 would bore other children of the same age. Abigail Sin practiced piano at least 25 hours a week. Similarly, two-year-old Nguyen Ngoc Truong Son had the **concentration** to play chess for hours at a time. The distinction of "prodigy" thus goes beyond

55 mere **intelligence**. For explanations, **experts** look in two directions: *nature*, the child's unique biology, and *nurture*, the child's **environment**.

When researchers look to *nature* to explain child prodigies, they study innate, or inborn,

60 qualities. For example, they look at whether the brain structure of a prodigy is different from that of a child with average **intelligence**. **Technology** is a great help in answering this question. For instance, scientists **utilize** imaging

65 **technology** to see the amount of activity in different parts of the brain. These brain scans **reveal** that the frontal lobe of a prodigy's brain is very active, unlike children with average **intelligence** doing the same tasks. Their frontal

70 lobes are virtually inactive. Science has proven that the frontal lobe of the brain controls many aspects of thought and **concentration**. This may explain how prodigies can **focus** on a task, solve complex problems, and learn quickly.

75 When researchers look to *nurture* to explain child prodigies, they **focus** on the child's **environment** instead of the child's biology. The most important **factor** on the *nurture* side is the parents. Raising a child prodigy is extremely

80 **challenging**. It requires **considerable** patience, creativity, and resourcefulness.

Some parents are delighted by the extraordinary abilities of their children. They make use of all the **resources** they have or can find to

85 support them. For example, Jay Greenberg's parents bought their two-year-old son a cello when he requested it and arranged for music lessons.

Other parents are not so supportive of their child prodigy. On the contrary, some parents

90 even see their offspring's gifts as a way to draw attention to themselves and their own interests. Boris Sidis, for example, was a well-known scientist with strong opinions about making the most of one's **intelligence** and about raising

95 children. When his son Billy was born, Boris saw the child as an opportunity to test his theories.

From Billy's birth, it was clear that he was an exceptional child. His parents **utilized** every opportunity to teach him language, math,

100 science, and logic. Boris was very poor, but he used his limited **resources** to buy or acquire toys and books for the young genius. Billy Sidis spoke five languages at age five. He passed entry exams for MIT and Harvard Medical

105 School at age nine and was admitted to Harvard at age 11. He was considered a genius in mathematics, physics, and languages.

Boris claimed that his methods of child-rearing were responsible for his son's abilities

110 and took his story to the press. The press, in turn, **focused** more on the young Harvard student's odd personal life than on his accomplishments. It was soon clear that Billy was unprepared to relate to other people, function successfully in the real

115 world, or manage the **challenges** of being different. After college, he lived an isolated life. Despite his **intelligence**, he died unemployed and in poverty.

When people are unusual, they attract attention. In the case of child prodigies, the

120 attention they receive is both positive and negative. It is positive because most people admire **intelligence**. It is negative because prodigies are very different from other people. They are a **challenge** for teachers, who expect seven-year-

125 olds to prefer Batman to Beethoven. They are a **challenge** to parents, who want to help them but often lack the **resources** or find their needs and desires difficult to understand and meet. They present a **challenge** to scientists, who want

130 to study them without further isolating them from **normal** society. And they **challenge** the world because they **reveal** the tendency that people have to reject those who are different from the norm. ■

# Reading Comprehension

Mark each sentence as *T* (true) or *F* (false) according to the information in Reading 1. Use the dictionary to help you understand new words.

___ 1. The parents of two-year-old Nguyen Ngoc Truong Son taught him to play chess, and he learned very quickly.

___ 2. The parents of Jay Greenberg did not provide an environment that was focused on music, but Jay had great interest in music at a very young age.

___ 3. Jay Greenberg wrote symphonies very quickly because he utilized the help of talented professional composers.

___ 4. The factors that seem to always be present in a child prodigy are 1) an unusually high intelligence and 2) the ability to master one area, such as music or math.

___ 5. The child prodigies mentioned in the reading showed considerable interest and ability in creative writing.

___ 6. Technology has revealed that the brains of highly intelligent children are different than the brains of children with normal intelligence.

___ 7. Child prodigies sometimes select areas of interest that they did not learn from their parents or their environment. This supports the explanation of *nurture*.

___ 8. All of the parents mentioned in the article provided their children with both educational and psychological resources.

___ 9. According to the article, people with normal intelligence present fewer challenges to society and are more accepted.

## READING SKILL · Recognizing Comparison and Contrast

### LEARN

Writers often compare things and ideas to show how they are similar. They also contrast things and ideas to show how they are different. Comparisons and contrasts are important in helping the reader understand how things and ideas relate to each other. You can recognize comparisons and contrasts by the context clues that signal them.

### APPLY

**A.** Read these context clues. Write *S* for those that indicate similarity (comparison) or *D* for those that indicate difference (contrast). Compare your answers with a partner.

| | | |
|---|---|---|
| _S_ both | ___ in the same way | ___ on the contrary |
| ___ but | ___ instead of | ___ on the other hand |
| ___ despite | ___ likewise | ___ similarly |
| ___ however | ___ moreover | ___ unlike |

Some words signal a contrast between the central meanings of two sentences. Careful reading will often reveal that *words* are also being contrasted.

> *Child prodigies attract <u>praise and attention</u> from everyone they meet; on the other hand, they attract <u>criticism</u>, and they find it difficult to fit in with the rest of the world.*

**B.** Look at these lines from Reading 1. Write the context clue and circle whether it indicates comparison or contrast. Then, write which words are being compared or contrasted.

1. Line 3

   Context clue: *however* _____ Comparison or (contrast?)

   Words: *normal / unusual* _____

2. Line 13

   Context clue: _____ Comparison or contrast?

   Words: _____

3. Line 33

   Context clue: _____ Comparison or contrast?

   Words: _____

4. Line 52

   Context clue: _____ Comparison or contrast?

   Words: _____

5. Line 68

   Context clue: _____ Comparison or contrast?

   Words: _____

6. Line 77

   Context clue: _____ Comparison or contrast?

   Words: _____

7. Line 89

   Context clue: _____ Comparison or contrast?

   Words: _____

## Vocabulary Activities  STEP I: Word Level

**A.** Read these excerpts from another article on child prodigies. For each excerpt, cross out the one word or phrase in parentheses with a different meaning from the other three choices. Compare your answers with a partner.

1. Parents can create a positive or a negative environment for their highly intelligent children. The mother of six-year-old Hungarian cellist Janos Starker wanted her son to (*display / concentrate on / focus on / think about*) his music practice, so she made tiny sandwiches and left them on his music stand. She didn't want him to have to get up and look for a snack.

2. Given the results, we should not be critical of this mother's methods. Janos Starker's (*considerable / great / expert / extensive*) success as an international cellist lasted over 50 years, and his is one of the great musical careers of our time.

3. Another musician to (*reveal / display / utilize / demonstrate*) exceptional musical promise was pianist Ruth Slezynska. She performed at a major concert for the first time in 1929 at the age of four.

4. Whereas Starker's mother encouraged him with tiny sandwiches, Slezynska's father created (*a feeling / an environment / an atmosphere / a setting*) of fear. He forced her to practice nine hours every day and hit her when she played a wrong note.

5. The abnormal (*isolation / anxiety / pressure / stress*) was too much for the young girl. At 15 she suffered a major breakdown that ended her career.

The word *resource(s)* refers to something that a person or a country can use. It can be tangible (money, equipment) or intangible (moral support, knowledge).

CORPUS

**B.** Which of these items would be useful resources for a doctor? Put a check (✓) next to these items. How might a doctor utilize each resource? Discuss your answers with a partner.

___ 1. books        ___ 5. a microscope

___ 2. a computer        ___ 6. a hammer

___ 3. another doctor in the family        ___ 7. knowledge of astronomy

___ 4. coal        ___ 8. a telephone

**C.** What are some resources that these people might utilize? Think of as many resources as possible. Discuss your answers in a small group.

1. marathon runner        3. business student

2. journalist        4. kindergarten teacher

To *reveal* something means "to make something known that was previously secret or unknown." A *revelation* is something important and usually surprising that is revealed.

CORPUS

**D.** With a partner, discuss these questions: What might each of these people *not* want to reveal? Why? What might result from the revelation?

1. a spy

2. a research scientist

3. a used-car salesman

4. a politician

5. a psychiatrist

| Word Form Chart | | | |
|---|---|---|---|
| **Noun** | **Verb** | **Adjective** | **Adverb** |
| challenge | challenge | challenging challenged* | _____ |

*When used as an adjective, *challenged* has a different meaning from the other words in its family. It means "having a particular type of difficulty" (for example, *visually challenged* or *physically challenged*). A synonym is *handicapped*. This form is not used in this unit.

**E.** Answer the questions using each form of *challenge* at least once. Refer to Reading 1 for information. Discuss your answers in a small group or as a class.

1. How did the Greenbergs feel about raising Jay?

   *For the Greenbergs, raising a child prodigy was a challenge, but they enjoyed*

   *supporting him and encouraging his interests.*

2. What were some of the difficulties faced by Billy Sidis in his adult life?

   _____

   _____

3. What difficulties do researchers or experts face as they try to better understand child prodigies?

   _____

   _____

4. What difficulties do child prodigies pose for society?

   _____

   _____

5. In your opinion, why do child prodigies "challenge the world" and the society they live in?

   _____

   _____

| Word Form Chart | | | |
|---|---|---|---|
| **Noun** | **Verb** | **Adjective** | **Adverb** |
| expertise expert | _____ | expert | expertly |
| _____ | _____ | considerable | considerably |
| technology technologist | _____ | technological | technologically |
| resource(s) | _____ | resourceful | resourcefully |

**F.** Read the story about another child prodigy, Chandra Sekar. Then restate each of the sentences in your notebook using the words in parentheses. Do not change the meanings of the sentences. Be prepared to share your work aloud.

1. Chandra Sekar grew up in India. Even though his family was too poor to own a computer, he was very interested in technology when he was a toddler. (*considerable, technological*)

   *Chandra Sekar didn't have a computer, but he showed considerable interest in technological things from a very early age.*

2. His father wanted to encourage Chandra's technological skills. (*technology*)

3. He hoped that Chandra would one day become a recognized expert in computers. (*expertise*)

4. His father was poor, but he found ways to earn enough money to buy the young boy a computer when he was only four years old. (*resourceful* or *resources*)

5. Chandra found a way to teach himself to use the operating system MS-DOS, and the computer programs LOTUS and MS-Word. (*technological resources* or *resourceful*)

6. He was only ten when he became the world's youngest Microsoft Certified Systems Engineer. The average age for engineers is 30. (*considerably*)

7. When he was 11 and a student at a university in Madras, the government of India honored Chandra because he was very knowledgeable about the technology related to computer network security. (*expertise* or *expert*)

**G.** Imagine you are a journalist and you have a chance to interview Chandra Sekar. Prepare interview questions using the cues provided. Record the questions in your notebook. Be prepared to act out your interview with a partner.

1. how / environment

   *How did your home environment help you succeed?*

2. which / factors

3. what / challenges

4. when / intelligent or intelligence

5. how / normal / different

6. who / influence

7. where / expertise

8. what / resources

9. why / concentrate or focus / technology

## Before You Read

**Read these questions. Discuss your answers in a small group.**

1. What do you think would be the biggest challenges for parents of a prodigy? Why do you think this is true?

2. Doctors and other experts claim that it is impossible for a child prodigy to live a "normal" life. What do you think they mean by this? Do you agree?

3. Children with high intelligence often score *lower* on standardized tests than do children of normal intelligence. Why do you think this happens?

## Read

This *New York Times* article gives advice to parents of child prodigies on how to meet the needs of their extraordinary children.

# Not Like Other Kids

Last summer, after serious thought, Toby Rosenberg announced to his friends and family that he was changing his name. "Toby," he felt, was "a little boy's name." Instead, he would be
5 called Karl, like his father before him. His school accepted the switch. His parents had no argument. Toby—now Karl—was five years old.

And he had a point: regardless of his age, Karl has never been a little boy. At 14 months, he
10 began to read aloud from the posters he viewed from his stroller. It would be another full year before he talked on his own; but once he did, he spoke fluent English and Polish (his mother, Anna, is from Krakow) and several other languages. He
15 trained himself to write Japanese after studying the label on a bottle. He taught himself the Hebrew alphabet after seeing the characters on a dreidel, a type of toy. Last year, after seeing a book in a museum shop on ancient Egypt, he
20 compiled a dictionary of hieroglyphics. The impression you get when you first meet Karl is that of a bookish teenager, a middle-aged diplomat, and a talkative grandmother trapped together in the body of a first-grader.

25 "You don't know what it's like with Karl," his father says, laughing tiredly. Karl Sr. was once an artist, and is now a website designer. He spends at least an hour every afternoon in the family's one-bedroom Brooklyn apartment
30 drafting sketches and submitting them to his son's critiques. "He stands behind me and tells me to draw things over and over to his specifications," Karl says. "If he's not on the Internet, he's here, issuing commands over my
35 shoulder. We just want to encourage his interests and support him any way we can. Nobody in this household is trying to tell him what to do." Which is just as it should be.

**Experts** offer parents of child prodigies this
40 advice about raising their gifted children:

**1. Don't overstructure your child's life.**
**Experts** advise parents of hyper-**intelligent** children that, instead of filling their time with planned activities, they should try not to be too
45 controlling. "Profoundly gifted kids are highly curious and likely to **pursue** all kinds of interests with great passion," says Sandra Berger, a gifted-education specialist for more

than 20 years. "It's best to let the child's interests be your guide."

### 2. Provide as many learning opportunities as possible.
Parents should strive to introduce their children to a wide variety of subjects. They should take them on field trips and museum tours; moreover, the child's **normal environment** should be treated as an experiential playground. It was reportedly his early walks in the woods with his father that alerted Richard Feynman, the Nobel-prize-winning physicist, to the complexity of life. For Karl, it was drives past the Williamsburg Bridge that piqued his avid interest in construction.

Such interests can prove a distraction. When he was taking his Educational Records Bureau exam in January, Karl spent much of the allotted time lecturing the test-givers on the unusual architecture of the Chrysler Building, which was visible through the classroom window. When the examiners tried to summarize Karl's irregular score, they mentioned his "most noteworthy…fund of knowledge."

Of course, even without a standardized-test score, Karl's parents know he's a genius. On the other hand, they know that they should never, ever use that term.

### 3. Avoid calling your child a genius.
"There are three reasons the label could only be unhelpful," says Dr. Jack Shonkoff, an **expert** on early childhood development. "One, it puts an **enormous** burden on the kid that he or she will have trouble living up to. Two, it's a setup for other people—relatives, teachers—to be disappointed in the kid's future performance. And three, it serves to set the child apart from other children." Shonkoff says that extremely talented kids are pigeonholed, or stereotyped, enough already. They don't need a label to isolate them even more.

### 4. Don't expect your child to be popular.
Combating social isolation may be the greatest **challenge** for those raising exceptionally **intelligent** kids. Karl has had a typically uphill battle finding a school—let alone a circle of friends—that can contain him. At three years old, he was asked to leave his preschool program at the local Y.M.C.A. His teachers thought that his obvious boredom was a bad influence on the other children. After a search, his parents discovered the East Manhattan School for Bright and Gifted Children, but the independent school soon closed. Karl then transferred to a first-grade class at a public school in Brooklyn. He was immediately promoted to its accelerated program, but his social life lagged far behind.

It's no surprise. Adults tend to make friendships on the basis of shared interests and coincidental **pursuits**. Similarly, highly gifted children seek out friends like themselves, rather than falling into groups according to age or grade. "These kids just aren't likely to be part of a huge gang in the lunchroom," Berger says.

### 5. Don't sacrifice educational advancement to give your child a "normal" upbringing.
Holding children back from upper-level grades and early college won't help them socially. On the contrary, it will frustrate them—and their teachers. "These kids will exhaust the **resources** of any **normal** classroom," Berger says. "Six-, seven-, and eight-year-olds who are interested in aerospace **technology** shouldn't be stuck in homeroom."[1]

Karl's extensive **pursuits** could exhaust just about anyone. He's played the piano since he was three. Two years later he requested a violin, and his parents managed to borrow one. In addition, the family's apartment was cluttered with Karl's drawings of the Titanic, which he reimagined as a medieval galleon, with his floor sculpture of Moscow's St. Basil's Cathedral reconfigured as an ancient Irish church and with the whirling presence of Karl himself.

Preparing to present his well-illustrated, self-assigned report on the Statue of Liberty, he announced to his family: "The architect was Frederic-Auguste Bartholdi; Auguste— I mean—did you hear that? A-goose. I said goose!" He bursts into giggles, and for the moment, at least, Karl Jr. is completely happy and six years old.

---

[1] *homeroom:* the room where children gather to start the school day and to wait for activities

# Reading Comprehension

Mark each sentence as *T* (true) or *F* (false) according to the information in Reading 2. Use the dictionary to help you understand new words.

___ 1. Toby Rosenberg pursued changing his name because he and his parents had a challenging relationship. They did not get along well.

___ 2. Karl Jr. learned languages before he went to school because his parents utilized the help of private tutors at home.

___ 3. Karl Jr.'s teachers believed that he was a bad influence on other children because he acted bored.

___ 4. Child prodigies usually have an enormous number of friends.

___ 5. Two factors that make life more challenging for bright children are isolation from other children their age and difficulty in finding an appropriate school.

___ 6. Intelligence comes naturally for child prodigies, but concentration does not.

___ 7. The article suggests that it is not necessary for parents to select new areas of interest for their children. Highly intelligent children do best when they are allowed to pursue their natural interests.

___ 8. Most classrooms don't have enough resources to meet the educational needs of exceptionally bright children.

## READING SKILL | Recognizing Comparison and Contrast

### APPLY

Skim Reading 2 for context clues and record them. Circle whether they indicate comparison or contrast, and write which words or ideas are being compared or contrasted. Compare your findings with a partner.

1. Line(s): *4*

   Context clue: *Instead*                    Comparison or ⟨contrast?⟩

   Words being compared/contrasted: *Toby, Karl*

2. Line(s): _____

   Context clue: _____    Comparison or contrast?

   Words being compared/contrasted: _____

3. Line(s): _____

   Context clue: _____    Comparison or contrast?

   Words being compared/contrasted: _____

4. Line(s): _____

   Context clue: _____    Comparison or contrast?

   Words being compared/contrasted: _____

5. Line(s): _____

   Context clue: _____    Comparison or contrast?

   Words being compared/contrasted: _____

What does Karl Sr. mean by "You don't know what it's like with Karl"? Why is he "laughing tiredly"? Support your inferences with information from Reading 2.

## Vocabulary Activities STEP I: Word Level

**A.** Complete the sentences about Albert Einstein using the target vocabulary in the box. Use each item one time. The synonyms in parentheses can help you.

| | | | |
|---|---|---|---|
| concentrated | an environment | intelligence | revealed |
| considerably | expertise | normal | |
| enormous | factor | pursued | |

___ a. The ___enormous___ _____ of Albert Einstein is now well
          (very large)       (mental ability)
known, but it wasn't so obvious when he was young.

___ b. In school, the young Einstein loved mathematics and science, but he

_____ less on other subjects. He received poor grades in
  (focused)
history, geography, and languages.

___ c. When he was 16, he wrote a paper that _____ his early ideas
                    (made known)
about the theory of relativity.

___ d. Though it is _____ for children to speak before the age of
          (usual)
three, Einstein didn't say his first words until he was nearly four. He didn't

read until he was seven, which was _____ older than other
                (much)
prodigies such as Abigail Sin or Billy Sidis.

___ e. As a boy, Einstein's two uncles gave him _____ that challenged
             (the surroundings)
him and encouraged his interest in mathematics and science.

___ f. His _____ related to his theory continued throughout his life.
     (knowledge)
He was awarded the Nobel Peace Prize in 1921.

___ g. One _____ that led to his interest in physics sprang from an
      (thing)
incident that occurred when he was only five. His uncles showed him a

compass. From then on, Einstein _____ physics with great
             (tried to understand)
passion.

**B.** Tell the story of Einstein's life by putting the sentences in activity A into a logical order. Number them from *1* to *7* (more than one sequence may be possible). Then, use the target words as you compare stories with a partner.

**C.** Many academic words are also considered formal words. Which of the target words in this unit (see the list on page 113) are more formal synonyms for these informal words? Be sure to use the right form of the target words.

**Informal**                                 **Formal**

1. smart                            _____

2. to use                           _____

3. huge                             _____

4. uncover                          _____

5. difficulty                       _____

6. (specialized) knowledge          _____

7. activities or pastimes           _____

A word analogy shows the relationship between two pairs of words. First, you identify the relationship between the first pair of words. The relationship is usually synonyms, antonyms, examples, or verb/object:

> concentrate : focus          synonyms
> heredity : environment       antonyms
> psychologist : expert        example
> focus : attention            verb/object

To complete an analogy, find a word for the second pair that shows the same relationship as in the first pair of words:

> concentrate : focus  AS  utilize : *use*

The analogy is read like this: "*Concentrate* is to *focus* as *utilize* is to *use*." This means that the word "concentrate" has the same relationship to the word "focus" as the word "utilize" has to the word "use." *Concentrate* and *utilize* are each a synonym for the other word.

CORPUS

**D.** Use target vocabulary from this unit (in the correct form) to complete these analogies. Then write the type of relationship each analogy has. Compare your work with a partner's.

**Type of relationship**

1. intelligent : unintelligent  AS  normal : *abnormal*          *antonyms*

2. a painting : art  AS  a computer : _____       _____

3. get : receive  AS  seek : _____       _____

4. car : transportation  AS  money : _____       _____

5. hide : reveal  AS  waste : _____       _____

6. show : respect  AS  focus : _____       _____

**E.** Read these sample sentences that feature the words *normal* and *norm* and answer the questions below in your notebook, using the dictionary as suggested. Compare your answers with a partner.

- Technology has revealed that the brains of highly intelligent children are different from the brains of children with normal intelligence.
- Child prodigies challenge the world because they reveal the tendency to reject people who seem too different from the norm.
- Experts claim that it is impossible for a child prodigy to live a "normal" life.
- A child prodigy's normal environment should be treated as an experiential playground.
- Don't sacrifice educational advancement to give your child a "normal" upbringing.

1. What are some things that are referred to as *normal* in the sample sentences?

2. Look up the word *normal* in your dictionary and read the sample sentences. What are some other things that are referred to as normal?

3. What is implied when *normal* appears in quotation marks?

4. What is meant by *the norm*? Write a brief definition. Confirm it with your dictionary.


## Vocabulary Activities  STEP II: Sentence Level

**F.** In a small group, discuss these questions. Use the dictionary to clarify word meanings, if needed.

1. Think about a culture that you know well. What are the norms for each of these customs? What factors might have caused these norms to develop?

   a. the food eaten for the evening meal

   b. the gifts that are given for a major holiday

   c. the age that young people move away from their families

   d. the amount of money spent on children's education

2. What do you think are the three most important factors to consider when parents are choosing a school for their child?

   ___ a. location

   ___ b. number of children in a class

   ___ c. friendly classroom environment

   ___ d. the intelligence of the teachers

   ___ e. the intelligence of the other students

   ___ f. the school's technological resources

   ___ g. the condition of the school building

   ___ h. other: _____

**G.** Which of these pursuits do you consider most challenging? Rank them from *1* (most challenging) to *4* (least challenging).

___ reading a book in Spanish      ___ fixing a broken computer

___ cooking dinner for ten people      ___ running a three-mile race

**As a class or in small groups, make a chart and tally everyone's answers. Which item does the group find most challenging? Least challenging? Why do you think this is true? What environmental factors do you think might have contributed to the results?**

Both hereditary and environmental factors have considerable influence on the person a child becomes. Hereditary factors include the biological traits that people inherit from their parents, such as eye color or height. Environmental factors refer to the things that happen to people after they are born: for example, the way their parents treat them, what they learn and experience, what they eat, where they live, and even illnesses or accidents that occur.

**H.** Read these factors that have shaped the lives of some child prodigies. Write *H* in the blank for those you think are hereditary factors. Write *E* for those you think are environmental factors. Then explain your answer and how each factor may have affected the child. Present your opinions in a small group.

___ 1. The parents of Nguyen Ngoc Truong Son make less than 100 U.S. dollars in a month.

_____

_____

___ 2. Jay Greenberg has "heard music in his head" since he was two years old.

_____

_____

___ 3. Abigail Sin has a twin brother who is not a child prodigy.

_____

_____

___ 4. Billy Sidis spoke five languages at the age of five, including his father's native Russian.

_____

_____

The verb *pursue* means "to follow something in order to catch it or to work at something in order to accomplish it."

> The police **pursued** the robber in a car chase.

The noun form, *pursuit*, is often followed by the preposition *of* and a noun.

> My parents are happy about my **pursuit** <u>of a career in business.</u>

CORPUS

**I.** Look at these arguments for and against government, or public, involvement in the education of child prodigies. Restate each idea in your notebook, using the word in parentheses. Then, write a paragraph that expresses your own opinion. Try to use as many target words as possible in your work. Be prepared to present your work in class.

| For | Against |
|---|---|
| All children should have the right to realize their highest potential. Therefore, public money should be spent to help prodigies achieve their goals. (*pursuit*) | Public resources are limited. We cannot afford to spend extra money to help child prodigies. (*pursuing*) |
| Prodigies are a valuable future resource for a society; therefore, the government should help them try to reach their intellectual goals. (*pursue*) | Very few people have prodigies in their families. It is therefore unfair to spend public funds and give special attention to them. (*resources*) |
| Prodigies are likely to achieve more if more resources are made available to them. Society should do everything in its power to help develop a prodigy's intellect and expertise. (*utilization*) | In the interest of equal education for all children, extra resources should not be given to child prodigies. Funds for education should be spent to improve education for all children. (*utilized*) |

**J.** Self-Assessment Review: Go back to page 113 and reassess your knowledge of the target vocabulary. How has your understanding of the words changed? What words do you feel most comfortable with now?

## Writing and Discussion Topics

**Write about or discuss the following topics.**

1. Interests and abilities seem to run in some families. Is this the result of environmental or hereditary factors? Comment on this using examples from your own experience and from the readings and exercises in this unit.

2. One study of 32 exceptional physics and chemistry students in Taiwan found that the most important factors in the development of their intellectual abilities were family size, family income, and the child's place in the birth order. That is, over 75 percent of these students were the firstborn child in a small family with a relatively high income. Why do you think this is true?

3. Sometimes a child prodigy is raised in a family with other siblings, making it difficult for the parents to maintain a family environment that meets all of the children's needs. What suggestions would you make to such a family to help them create a suitable home environment for all of the children? Consider such factors as family routines, household rules, and discipline.

# The Competitive Instinct

## In this unit, you will

> read about how human competition has shaped business and culture over time.

> review summarizing a text using nontext elements.

> increase your understanding of the target academic words for this unit.

**READING SKILL** Understanding Time Signals

## Self-Assessment

Think about how well you know each target word, and check (✓) the appropriate column. I have…

| TARGET WORDS | never seen the word before | seen the word but am not sure what it means | seen the word and understand what it means | used the word, but am not sure if correctly | used the word confidently in *either* speaking *or* writing | used the word confidently in *both* speaking *and* writing |
|---|---|---|---|---|---|---|
| **AWL** | | | | | | |
| 🔑 behalf | | | | | | |
| 🔑 classic | | | | | | |
| commence | | | | | | |
| 🔑 commission | | | | | | |
| 🔑 contract | | | | | | |
| correspond | | | | | | |
| currency | | | | | | |
| 🔑 devote | | | | | | |
| flexible | | | | | | |
| 🔑 license | | | | | | |
| mechanism | | | | | | |
| 🔑 parallel | | | | | | |
| portion | | | | | | |
| 🔑 principle | | | | | | |
| qualitative | | | | | | |

🔑 Oxford 3000™ keywords

## Before You Read

Read these questions. Discuss your answers in a small group.

1. Do you consider yourself to be a competitive person? Why or why not?

2. Do you think the urge to compete is something people are born with or something they learn from their parents? Why?

3. Does society have an effect on an individual's competitive drive? If so, how? Are some societies more competitive than others? Give examples to support your opinions.

### MORE WORDS YOU'LL NEED

**instinct:** the natural force that causes a person or animal to behave in a certain way without thinking about it.

## Read

This article is a timeline that traces the history of competition—personal, professional, and national.

# The Competitive Edge: A Timeline of Human Ingenuity

Are you a runner? A soccer player? Have you ever competed in a sport, felt the thrill of the game, or raced for the win? Why is it that our best performances are often those played against
5 our toughest competitors? Ask Liliya Shobukhova (top right) of Russia when she attained her best marathon time. She won't tell you she did it while training alone. She did it while running—and winning—the 2011 Chicago Marathon, her third
10 consecutive win. It's not just physical competition that inspires us. As many of us can testify, competition affects every aspect of life. The following timeline demonstrates that the competitive instinct has been around for a long
15 time and has produced some staggering results.

### ANCIENT HISTORY
### THE STORIES WE TELL

Before written language developed, oral stories were handed down from one generation to the next. From Greek mythology to the plays of Shakespeare, **classical** literature abounds with
20 tales of rivalry between siblings. Often birth order, gender, and status within the family play into the clashes as siblings determine the best strategy for succeeding over the other. Whether it's for parental approval, wealth, or love, competition
25 between siblings is an age-old story. It's a drama we don't tire of easily.

### 1206
### THE LARGEST EMPIRE

A boy abandoned in the Mongolian grasslands with his mother and siblings later controls the largest empire in history. As a warrior, he
30 conquers the tribes competing for control of Mongolia and brings them under his rule, thereby earning the title "Genghis Khan," which means "ruler of all between the oceans." Now acknowledged as a leader, he **commences**

35 a lifelong career of brutal military campaigns. Throughout his reign, Khan commands a network of armies in different regions, all fighting on his **behalf**. He uses songs to communicate plans of attack to a largely illiterate officer group. These
40 rhymes help soldiers remember and execute orders. Even now, stories of this legendary man continue to make the news.

## 1296
## AN ENGINEERING FEAT

In an effort to compete with the beauty of the cathedrals in Pisa and Sienna, the Florentine
45 elite **commission** Arnolfo di Cambio to build a great cathedral. He builds a nave[1] so large, no one is certain how to construct a dome over it. Not until the fourteenth century is the problem solved. This time a competition is held to see
50 who can devise a strategy to complete the dome. Filippo Brunelleschi wins the competition with his ingenious design. He uses a system of interlocking bricks so the structure can support itself. This engineering feat ushers in
55 the Renaissance.[2]

## 1419
## GETTING THERE FIRST

Prince Henry the Navigator of Portugal begins sending regular expeditions to the coast of Africa, eventually reaching the Indian Ocean. Henry's **devotion** to exploration leads to competition
60 between Spain and Portugal. Over the next 150 years, both countries send out Atlantic voyages that bring Europeans to the Americas.

## 1450
## THE PATH TO LITERACY

Starting with the Chinese in the ninth century, who used blocks of wood to imprint characters
65 on paper, printing is used to create **currency** and books. However, it is not until 1450 that the world sees the first book printed using moveable metal type. Soon after Johannes Gutenberg establishes his press in Germany, other
70 European countries want their own. With books becoming widely available, the printing press is credited with an increase in the number of schools, a **corresponding** steep rise in literacy, and consequently the creation of the
75 middle class.

## 1854
## COMPETITION OF MARKETS

In 1854, William Makepeace Thackeray uses the term *capitalism,* meaning "having ownership of capital," in his novel *The Newcomers*. The meaning and term evolve to encapsulate the economic
80 **principles** we associate with it: private ownership of production, goods, and services, and the ability for businesses to compete for profit in free markets. Proponents of the system argue that competition leads to better quality and lower
85 prices. Opponents point to its role in class division and an unequal distribution of wealth.

## 1957
## THE SPACE RACE

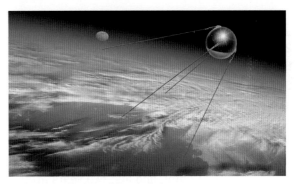

Artist's rendering of Sputnik I

The Soviet Union[3] launches Sputnik I, the first satellite. This satellite, about the size of a beach ball, sparks The Space Race between
90 the United States and the Soviet Union. The space programs of the United States and the Soviet Union **parallel** each other in this race to be the first to reach the moon. Billions of dollars in aerospace research are spent by

---

[1] *nave:* the main interior part of a church, which extends from the entry to the altar
[2] *Renaissance:* a time period in the fourteenth to sixteenth century marked by a renewed interest in ancient Greek and Roman learning and cultural transformation of the times, beginning in Italy and spreading across Europe
[3] *The Soviet Union:* a group of countries that formerly existed as a single political body in eastern Europe and northern Asia, led by Russia and including Ukraine, Lithuania, Kazakhstan, and others

each. The United States reaches the moon first, in 1969.

---

*1980*

## THE PERSONAL COMPUTER

Company executives from IBM schedule a visit with Gary Kildall at his company, Digital Research. They want to **license** his operating system in IBM's new personal computer. According to legend, Kildall decides to take a flight on his private plane instead of meeting with IBM, but he doesn't cancel the appointment. The IBM executives come to Digital Research, but Kildall is not there. A young self-starter named Bill Gates reportedly says, "Gary went flying." Gates then offers to let them license his DOS system instead. IBM agrees, and soon Bill Gates and Microsoft are household names. There are several variations on this story, but most report that Kildall did fly his plane that day; however, it was to a previously scheduled meeting with an important customer, not just a trip for fun. The phrase "Gary went flying" stuck though, and has become an industry phrase meaning "a great, lost opportunity."

---

*2004*

## BUILDINGS THAT SCRAPE THE SKY

Cy Lee designs Taipei 101, a 101-story skyscraper that becomes the world's highest structure, a record previously held for 30 years by the Willis Tower in Chicago. But four years later, the Taipei record is beaten by the Shanghai World Financial Center, and just two years after that by Burj Khalifa in Dubai. However, in 2011, **contracts** are signed for a tower in Saudi Arabia even taller than Burj Khalifa.

**Taipei 101 was the world's tallest building for only four years.**

---

*2010*

## TESTING, TESTING . . .

The results of the 2009 PISA (Program for International Student Assessment) are released. The test, a **mechanism** for measuring skills in reading, math, and science, is administered to 15-year-old students in 65 countries. Students in Shanghai, China, outperform the rest of the world. Other countries begin both **qualitative** and quantitative analysis to prove the educational abilities of their students.

---

*2011*

## GOING GREEN

On October 31, 2011, the United Nations estimates that the world population has reached seven billion. Editorials fill the world's newspapers with solutions to the world's depleting resources as more and more people compete for their **portion** of food, energy, and wealth. Previously, the United Nations had predicted the world wouldn't reach seven billion until 2013. Companies continue to search for viable ways to supply energy to the world's growing population. Only the future will tell what innovations this competition yields.

# Reading Comprehension

**Read each sentence below. Choose the best answer to complete the sentence based on Reading 1.**

1. According to the section "The Stories We Tell," humans have a long history of telling stories about _____ .

   a. physical competition of athletes

   b. the path to literacy

   c. competition between siblings

2. Using rhymes to help soldiers remember and follow through on orders was a strategy _____ used.

   a. Filippo Brunelleschi

   b. Genghis Khan

   c. Prince Henry the Navigator

3. Capitalism is associated with competition because _____ .

   a. businesses are allowed to compete

   b. William Makepeace Thackeray used the term

   c. it leads to better quality and lower prices

4. The Space Race refers to _____ .

   a. the launch of Sputnik I by the Soviet Union

   b. the Soviet Union and United States' race to reach the moon

   c. the Soviet Union and United States' race to launch a satellite

5. Gary Kildall was _____ .

   a. the owner of Digital Research

   b. an IBM executive

   c. a phrase used within the computer industry

6. The _____ held the record for 30 years for being the tallest building in the world.

   a. Taipei 101

   b. Shanghai World Financial Center

   c. Willis Tower

7. The PISA _____ .

   a. is a tower planned to go up in Saudi Arabia

   b. measures reading, math, and science skills

   c. is the name of a satellite

8. As the population increases, companies _____ .

   a. compete for their portion of resources

   b. predict that newspapers will offer solutions

   c. search for new ways to supply energy

## LEARN

Although timelines present historical information, they are often written in the present tense. This makes the information seem more interesting and immediate, but it also makes the use of time words very important.

These time words and expressions can be found in this reading:

| | | | |
|---|---|---|---|
| throughout | soon | starting with | eventually |
| for...years | over the next | then | previously |
| later | in (+ year) | even now | after that |

## APPLY

Look back at the timeline and underline the time expressions.

### REVIEW A SKILL  Summarizing a Text Using Nontext Elements (See p. 69)

When you summarize information, you need to figure out the main ideas of a selection and combine them briefly and clearly. As you complete the activity below, review each section of the timeline and identify the main ideas.

In your notebook, record the dates for each event given in Reading 1. Then summarize each section as briefly as you can and still record the important facts. Use the present tense and include time words as necessary to clarify the sequence of events. Compare your work in a small group.

## Vocabulary Activities  STEP I: Word Level

**A.** Read the sentences. Circle the sentence with the same meaning. Use a dictionary to help you.

1. The council **commissioned** the large sculpture.

   a. The council admired the large sculpture.

   b. The council paid for the large sculpture.

   c. The council tore down the large sculpture.

2. The artist **commenced** work the next day.

   a. The artist finished work the next day.

   b. The artist commented on the work the next day.

   c. The artist began work the next day.

3. The city established a **mechanism** for reporting problems.

   a. The city established a system for reporting problems.

   b. The city established a machine for reporting problems.

   c. The city established a new contract for reporting problems.

4. The two companies signed a **contract.**

   a. The two companies signed an application.

   b. The two companies signed an agreement.

   c. The two companies signed a petition.

5. He acted on his father's **behalf.**

   a. He represented his father.

   b. He helped his father.

   c. He worked for his father.

6. At that school, they evaluate students **qualitatively.**

   a. At that school, they evaluate based on students' percentages.

   b. At that school, they evaluate with a description of students' performance.

   c. At that school, they evaluate students very strictly.

**B.** Read these excerpts from a text on business. For each excerpt, cross out the one word or phrase in parentheses with a different meaning from the other three choices. Compare your answers with a partner.

1. Patagonia, Inc., an outdoor equipment company in California, differs from the (*traditional / classical / established / innovative*) business model because it focuses on saving the environment rather than increasing profits.

2. Many creative workers come to Patagonia because they are interested in working for a company that values its (*consumers / morals / values / principles*) more than its profits.

3. Patagonia also has (*flexible / demanding / adaptable / changeable*) work hours for its employees, who are encouraged to spend a (*majority / part / portion / segment*) of their workday at the beach when conditions are good for surfing.

4. The company sees professional work and outdoor hobbies not as conflicting demands, but as complementary and (*helpful / equivalent / parallel / similar*) activities.

5. The founder and chairman of Patagonia, Yvon Chouinard, believes that (*devotion / attraction / commitment / dedication*) to recreation encourages innovation in product development.

6. Chouinard believes that the company's success and profitability (*corresponds to / is consistent with / is greater than / is related to*) its devotion to the environment and sustainable business practices.

**C.** Which of these jobs should require a license? Put a check (✓) next to them. Then, discuss your ideas in a small group. Together, decide which three are the most important to license, and share your ideas with the class.

___ driving a taxi       ___ building houses

___ operating a beauty salon       ___ practicing law (being a lawyer)

___ selling medicine       ___ taking care of pets

___ teaching children       ___ selling food to the public

## Vocabulary Activities   STEP II: Sentence Level

The adjective *qualitative* refers to an evaluation of something based on how good it is or on observations of different qualities. It can also be used to refer to evaluations based on observations rather than measurements.

> A **qualitative** study of employee satisfaction found that 75 percent of workers feel less loyalty to their companies now than they did ten years ago.

Note, the opposite of qualitative is *quantitative*, referring to evaluations using numbers and statistics.

CORPUS

**D.** Decide whether each item in the chart is a qualitative or quantitative evaluation. Explain your answers.

| | Qualitative | Quantitative |
|---|---|---|
| 1. 98% of customers that use products from the German software company SAP also use Microsoft Office. | | The percentage shows that this is purely a quantitative evaluation. |
| 2. Cirque de Soleil's success is due to its unique combination of circus and theater. | | |
| 3. 14% of new business is in new markets, which generates 61% of profits. | | |
| 4. Heavy equipment seller Caterpillar saw its profits increase by 38%. | | |
| 5. People see the grocery store Whole Foods as representative of a healthy, eco-friendly lifestyle. | | |

**E.** Read this story about business in China. Then, go back and restate each of the sentences in your notebook using the words in parentheses. Do not change the meanings of the sentences.

1. Traditionally, recent graduates face the problem of a difficult job search, but that was not Carmen Tan's problem. (*classic*)

   *The classic problem for recent graduates is a difficult job search, but that was not Carmen Tan's problem.*

2. Tan agreed to work for a particular major international company, although she could have begun her career with almost any company in China. (*contract; commenced*)

3. Companies doing business in China are so desperate to find well-trained employees that they offer many incentives, such as allowing employees to work the hours they want to and helping them get professional certification. (*flexible; licenses*)

4. Companies don't offer these benefits because they believe that workers should be well treated. (*principle*)

5. Rather, they hope that employees will reward them by being loyal and staying with the company for a long time. (*devotion*)

6. Companies in China have developed procedures through which younger workers often rise more quickly into leadership positions than young people on similar tracks in the West. (*mechanisms; parallel*)

7. These companies also offer different amounts of money as a reward for work of appropriate value. For example, they might award an employee 100 U.S. dollars to take the family out for dinner after completing a project. (*corresponding; currency*)

8. The success of Tan's new employer in attracting and keeping employees is partly due to the benefits it offers that can't be quantified. The company works hard to make employees feel recognized and appreciated. (*portion; qualitative*)

## Before You Read

Read these questions. Discuss your answers in a small group.

1. Think about products that you have used since you were a child. Do you have a favorite soft drink or cereal? Why do you buy these particular brands?

2. Now think about the companies that make those products. What do you know about the company? Why do you like their products?

3. What do you think is the best-selling brand or company in today's market? Why do you think other people like it?

## Read

This online article gives a brief account of the rise of brand names in the marketplace.

# Building a Competitive Brand

What's your next purchase going to be? Think. Did you think of a product, such as a new teapot or sweater? Or did you just think of a company name?

5 Maybe you are planning on getting the next Apple iPhone or taking a quick shopping trip to your favorite store. Perhaps you really like the company that makes the product. In fact, maybe you choose what you are going to buy based on
10 the brand name. If your response was more in line with the latter, your answer confirms what businesses already know: they are selling brands, not products.

The history of business goes hand in hand with
15 the history of marketing. If you have something to sell, you need to make people aware of it. As more businesses begin to sell the same product, competition for customers for that product increases. Whether it's another restaurant, type
20 of shoe, or lemonade stand, you need to market your product and position it so people know why they should buy it instead of another. Corporate logos can be traced back to the 1880s when businesses attached a personality to their
25 product. However, many point to the introduction of television in the 1950s and 60s as the

beginning of modern advertising. Suddenly, businesses had a captive audience to market to. With a small selection of TV channels
30 available, businesses could reach large audiences. For instance, in the United States, more than 50 percent of the population might be watching The Ed Sullivan Show on a given night. Company logos reached iconic status
35 during the 50s and 60s. Think of the red and white Coke label or the competing Pepsi symbol. Both soft drink companies have created
40 images that have become so well known, they are part of our print literacy.

45 The 1980s and 1990s brought another revolutionary change to product
50 competition and marketing. Cable and satellite TV

**Some brands, like Coke, span generations.**

increased the number of channels and programs available to people. The large audiences became
55 fragmented. Businesses could only count on events like the World Cup for a guaranteed mass viewing audience. Marketing became even more essential. The over hundred-year rivalry between Coke and Pepsi heated up. Businesses competed
60 for consumers by attaching more and more famous names to their product. TV ads became savvy, funny, interesting. Audiences began to look forward to commercial breaks during huge events like the Super Bowl or World Cup as part
65 of the entertainment.

But businesses also begin to recognize something else: branding is more than **licensing** a logo, more than a good laugh in a thirty-second TV spot. It's about establishing a real relationship
70 with the consumer and establishing a reputation. Why is it that the world consumes more than a billion Cokes each day? Coke has been able to enter foreign markets and compete with local products. Part of this is due to the company's
75 ability to advertise locally. In cities in South Africa, for example, a relatively new market for Coke, nearly every store has a Coke sign. The other part of this equation is not *how the company advertises*, but *what the company does*.
80 Coke sponsors sports events, economic development, scholarships, and other education projects. It's establishing itself in South Africa as a business with a conscience and a company that lends a helping hand.

85 In the 1990s, Nike, a sporting goods and clothing company, learned the importance of competing with a conscience when people found out that their products were being manufactured in sweatshops.[1] Consumers were angry. They didn't want to buy from
90 a company that supported child labor and unhealthy work conditions. Since then, Nike has had to invest a lot of money in rebuilding its reputation.

And rebranding a company takes a lot of money. Just ask Apple, a leader in computer, phone, and
95 music technology. During the late 1980s and 1990s, Apple increased its advertising budget

from 15 million to 100 million U.S. dollars. As a consequence, Apple became the biggest computer company in the world. Apple
100 changed its logo and message. It built an advertising campaign centered on people. Marc Gobe, author of *Emotional Branding*, described Apple this way to *Wired* magazine: "It's like having a good friend. That's what's
105 interesting about this brand. Somewhere they have created this really humanistic, beyond-business relationship with users and created a cult-like relationship with their brand. It's a big tribe, everyone is one of them. You're part
110 of the brand." Like Apple, other companies recognize the bond that people form with certain brands. For instance, the Swedish furniture company IKEA produces the most widely read catalog in the world. This company
115 has become a big hit in Europe and Africa, where the blue and yellow IKEA logo represents modern furniture design at an affordable cost. The Korean electronics company Samsung has also recognized the
120 importance of establishing a quality brand. In the early 2000s, it invested money in its product design and saw results in consumer approval. In this case it's **qualitative,** not quantitative, analysis that helps businesses
125 determine the consumers' regard for the brand. Essentially, it's how the consumer feels about the brand that sets the price a product will sell for. Naomi Klein, author of the book *No Logo*, best summarizes the
130 phenomenon of branding: "Brands conjure a feeling." They have an identity, and people define themselves through these brands.

As media and technology progress into the twenty-first century, with audiences now
135 streaming movies and shows online, it's not just **flexibility** that companies need to respond to via the changing media. To stay competitive, companies need to recognize the deep emotion that people have over brands,
140 and they need the innovation to inspire it.

---

[1] *sweatshops:* a term for workplaces, usually factories, that employ people for long hours for low pay; often associated with unhealthy working conditions and employing children illegally

# Reading Comprehension

Mark each statement as *T* (true) or *F* (false) according to the information in Reading 2. Then correct each false statement on the line below it.

___ 1. Companies realize they are selling products, not brands.

_____

___ 2. Corporate logos can be traced back to the 1960s.

_____

___ 3. When the number of TV channels available was low, advertising power was great.

_____

___ 4. In the 1980s and 1990s, it became more difficult for businesses to reach large audiences.

_____

___ 5. Branding means licensing a logo.

_____

___ 6. In order to sell its product, Coke sponsors educational projects.

_____

___ 7. Nike and Apple have both invested a lot of money in remaking their brand.

_____

___ 8. Samsung invested money into the quality design of its furniture.

_____

## READING SKILL    Understanding Time Signals

### APPLY

Read the article on pages 138–139 again. As you read, take notes in timeline form in your notebook. Choose a date that corresponds to the major events discussed. Then summarize each section, recording only the important information. Use the narrative present and include time words as necessary. Compare your work in a small group.

**A.** Read this passage about competition. Complete the sentences with target words from the box.

| | | | |
|---|---|---|---|
| commence | correspond | mechanism | parallels |
| commissions | devote | on behalf of | principle |

Competition is a basic part of the human experience and shows up in many aspects of life. The drive to make a goal and win the game has (1) _____ in the drive to make money and succeed at business or make good grades and be the top student in class. When employees or students are offered competitive rewards, a battle may (2) _____ that is not unlike the battle on the soccer field.

For many people, competition is an end in itself, and the drive to compete doesn't necessarily (3) _____ to the importance of the desired goal. The (4) _____ that controls competition in the human brain works just as well with sports and business as it does with things that are essential to survival. The urge is so strong that governments have had to create (5) _____ to oversee mergers and prevent monopolies.

However, no matter how strong a human's desire to compete is, competition obviously doesn't tell the whole story. Our emotional bonds with others often result in *altruism*, or actions that benefit others more than oneself. Some individuals (6) _____ their whole lives to improving work conditions, for example. Others fight injustice (7) _____ those who cannot speak for themselves. This altruistic (8) _____ helps balance the competitive instinct and drive people toward cooperation.

The word *commission* has two meanings. In one meaning, the verb means "to ask someone to do a piece of work." It can refer to a work of art, a study, or a special project of any sort. A *commission* is the result.

> They **commissioned** a study to gather evidence on how computer usage affects arm muscles.

> She received the **commission** to paint the CEO's portrait.

A *commission* can also refer to a group of people who are given official responsibility to regulate or investigate something. A *commissioner* is the leader of a commission.

> The Competition **Commission** is a British governmental organization that monitors British companies to make sure they are competing fairly.

CORPUS

**B.** With a partner, look at these commissions and discuss them. What might each commission regulate or investigate? Is a commission necessary to regulate these areas? Why or why not?

1. Commission on Human Rights
2. Parks and Recreation Commission
3. International Trade Commission
4. Commission on Ocean Policy
5. Atomic Energy Commission
6. Fish and Wildlife Commission

The word *currency* usually refers to different types of money. It can also refer to anything that is acting as a mechanism for exchange, or to anything that has abstract value in a certain situation.

> You can trade euros for yen at the **currency** exchange. (type of money)

> In the Internet world, information is the most valuable **currency**. (something of value)

> Managers resisted the new hiring policy at first, but it has gained **currency** lately. Now, they agree it's the best system. (abstract value)

CORPUS

**C.** In what situations might these things be used as currency? Use your imagination and think of one or two situations for each. Discuss your ideas in a small group.

1. information
2. airplane tickets
3. a car
4. the ability to speak another language
5. silence
6. a cell phone

**D.** Read the story about sports and management. Then, go back and restate each of the sentences in your notebook using the words in parentheses as indicated. Do not change the meanings of the sentences.

1. Theories of business management are being applied to other areas with great success. (*principles*)

   *Principles of business management are being successfully applied to other areas.*

2. The coach of one soccer team had been following a traditional model of team leadership by making his best players into team captains. Unfortunately, their leadership ability did not equal their sports skills. (*classic, correspond*)

3. The coach, Sasho Cirovski, saw similarities between what he needed and his brother Vancho's work in human resources. He decided to begin the next practice with a survey that Vancho used for organizational development. (*parallels, commence*)

4. The survey asked team members to associate descriptive characteristics with individuals on the team, for example, by identifying those who helped them increase their commitment to the team. (*qualitative, devotion*)

5. Based on the results of the survey, Coach Cirovski discovered that a player he had not seen as a leader, Scott Buete, had the respect of the team. Cirovski decided that he should be more adaptable in his selection of team leaders. He made an agreement with Buete that he would become a third team captain. (*flexible, contract*)

6. For the remaining part of the season, the team played much better. It seemed that Cirovski had finally found the right system for choosing a leader. (*portion, mechanism*)

*Devotion* refers to commitment, love, or dedication. If people are *devoted* to something, they are committed to it. If they are *devoted* to someone, that usually means that they love that person.

   *A good soccer player should be **devoted** to her team.*

To *devote time to* or *devote money to* something is another way of saying *spend time on* or *spend money on* something.

   *A good player **devotes** <u>a lot of time and energy to</u> practice.*

CORPUS

**E.** In your notebook, restate these sentences to include *devote*. Use each form at least once in your sentences. Compare your sentences with a partner.

1. Businesses used to expect a strong commitment from their employees.

   *Businesses used to expect devotion to the company from their employees.*

2. Nowadays, employees are rarely so attached to their company that they stay longer than a few years.

3. Many employees leave companies because they are expected to spend a lot of time on work-related projects.

4. They believe that companies should not expect employees to be loyal when they are asked to do an increasing amount of work.

5. At first, some businesses spent more money to try to get employees to stay with the company.

6. Now, however, most businesses have decided that they can't afford to buy the affection of their employees.

7. Instead of expecting company loyalty, they now expect employees to leave after a certain time and to get a regular number of new employees.

**F.** What do you think is important in a business manager? Rank these qualities from *1* (most important) to *8* (least important). Then write a paragraph in your notebook in which you explain your ranking. Be prepared to read aloud or discuss your ideas with the class.

___ highly principled        ___ honest

___ devoted to employees      ___ flexible

___ devoted to company       ___ focused on classic,
                                             time-honored strategies

___ well paid in relation
      to other employees        ___ innovative thinker

**G.** Self-Assessment Review: Go back to page 129 and reassess your knowledge of the target vocabulary. How has your understanding of the words changed? What words do you feel most comfortable with now?

## Writing and Discussion Topics

Write about or discuss the following topics.

1. Which do you think is a stronger instinct, cooperation or competition? Explain your answer with personal experience and ideas and examples from this unit.

2. What do you think is better for business, employees who stay at one company for a long time, or employees who work at many companies over their lifetimes? Why?

3. Is it better to evaluate employees qualitatively (for example, by describing their work style, accomplishments, etc.) or quantitatively (for example, by assigning them a number that reflects their skills and abilities)?

# UNIT
# 10

# Getting There

## In this unit, you will

> read about the latest developments in global navigation.
> review understanding time signals.
> utilize online encyclopedias.
> increase your understanding of the target academic words for this unit.

**READING SKILL** Identifying and Understanding Metaphors

## Self-Assessment

Think about how well you know each target word, and check (✓) the appropriate column. I have…

| TARGET WORDS | never seen the word before | seen the word but am not sure what it means | seen the word and understand what it means | used the word, but am not sure if correctly | used the word confidently in *either* speaking *or* writing | used the word confidently in *both* speaking *and* writing |
|---|---|---|---|---|---|---|
| **AWL** | | | | | | |
| assemble | | | | | | |
| attribute | | | | | | |
| 🔑 chart | | | | | | |
| 🔑 crucial | | | | | | |
| 🔑 enable | | | | | | |
| 🔑 equivalent | | | | | | |
| incidence | | | | | | |
| 🔑 item | | | | | | |
| manual | | | | | | |
| 🔑 precise | | | | | | |
| prohibit | | | | | | |
| 🔑 significant | | | | | | |
| 🔑 target | | | | | | |
| 🔑 vary | | | | | | |

🔑 Oxford 3000™ keywords

 **Outside the Reading** What do you know about location tracking?
Watch the video on the student website to find out more.

## Before You Read

**Read these questions. Discuss your answers in a small group.**

1. How did you learn to get around on your own in your city? When did you first go somewhere without an adult to lead the way? Where did you go? How did you find your way?

2. What's the hardest thing about finding your way around a new city? In a new place, do you find it more difficult to drive or take mass transit? Why?

3. Are you good at reading maps? Give an example to support your answer. Would you like to have a device that showed you or told you where to go each step of the way? Why or why not? If you already have a GPS device, how do you like it?

### MORE WORDS YOU'LL NEED

**cartographer:** one who makes maps
**cartography:** the science or art of making maps
**GPS:** Global Positioning System: a navigational system using satellites to identify locations
**navigate:** to decide on and steer a course, to make one's way over or through something

## READING SKILL  Identifying and Understanding Metaphors

### LEARN

A *metaphor* is a descriptive expression. It is a word or phrase from another context that replaces a more ordinary word or phrase in a text. This change of context suggests a comparison of the two things. Metaphors are more symbolic than direct comparisons and usually evoke an image for the reader.

> *The cow stood grazing alongside <u>the lunar landscape of potholes</u> that formed the only road in the region.*

By calling the road a "lunar landscape," the writer evokes an image of the surface of the moon. This comparison helps the reader imagine the appearance and condition of the road.

### APPLY

As you read, notice the metaphors the author uses. They have been underlined for your reference.

# Getting There:
# The Science of Driving Directions

## by Nick Paumgarten

In the fifteenth century, Henry the Navigator, a Portuguese prince, presided over a court in Sagres that became a center for cartographers, instrument-makers, and
5 explorers, whose expeditions he sponsored. Seafarers returning to Sagres from the west coast of Africa reported their discoveries, and new maps were produced, extending the reaches of the known world. These maps
10 became very valuable, owing to their utility in trade, war, and religious expansion, and were jealously guarded as state secrets.

Today's **equivalent** is a company called Navteq. It is the leading provider of geographic
15 data to the Internet mapping sites and the personal-navigation industry—the boiler room of the where-you-are-and-what-to-do business. Its biggest competitor has been a Dutch company called Tele Atlas. Most of the websites, car
20 manufacturers, and gadget-makers get the bulk of their raw material from these two companies. The

A GPS device

clients differ mainly in how they choose to present the data. This allows civilians[1] to have preferences.

Despite the digitization of maps and the
25 satellites circling the earth, the cartographic revolution still relies heavily on fresh observations made by people. Navteq, like Prince Henry, produces updates periodically (usually four times a year) for its corporate
30 clients. Its explorers are its geographic analysts. These people go onto the roads to make sure everything that the satellite data says about those roads is true—to check the old routes and record the new ones. The practice is called
35 ground-truthing. The analysts drive around and take note of what they call "**attributes**," which are anything of **significance** to a traveler seeking his way. A road segment can have one hundred sixty **attributes**, everything from a
40 speed limit to a drawbridge, an on-ramp,[2] or a **prohibition** against U-turns.[3] New signs, new roads, new exits, new rules: if such alterations go uncollected by Navteq, the traveler, relying on a device or a map produced by one of
45 Navteq's clients, might well get lost or confused. A driver making a simple left turn can encounter a blizzard of **attributes**: one-way, speed limit, crosswalk, traffic light, street sign, turn restriction, two-way, hydrant.
50 Navteq has more than six hundred field researchers and offices in many countries. In 2006, there were nine field researchers in the New York metropolitan area. One morning in fall, I went out with a pair of them, Chris Arcari
55 and Shovie Singh. "We're going to be working over by LaGuardia Airport," Arcari said. "One of the **items** we need to check out is some street

[1] *civilians:* people not connected with a particular area of interest
[2] *on-ramp:* the approach to a highway
[3] *U-turns:* turns that takes a driver in the opposite direction

names. They've put up new signs. Then we'll proceed to an area that we have **targeted**."

60 Arcari, who was brought up on Long Island, was the senior member of the team, and he tended to speak in the formal, polite, and indirect manner of a police officer testifying in court. He'd been with Navteq for ten years. Singh, who

65 grew up in Queens, New York, was a new hire. He'd got hooked on geography after taking some classes in the subject in college.

They were, you might say, free-driving—no navigation device or map—because they are not

70 only locals but also professionals in the New York-area discipline of getting from here to there. They spend two to three days a week just driving around. Manhattan's grid may be the easiest road network to master in the developed

75 world (if we overlook some areas), yet the routes leading to and from it can be tricky. The highways are <u>a mad thatch of interstates, parkways, boulevards, and spurs</u>, plus river crossings galore, each with its own virtues and

80 inconveniences. There are many ways to get from point A to point B in New York, and, because of all the **variations**, anyone can be a route-selection expert, or at least an enthusiast. Family gatherings inevitably feature relatives

85 eating cocktail nuts and arguing over the merits of various exits and shortcuts.

Eventually, we pulled into a gas station near the airport. Singh and Arcari **assembled** their equipment. They mounted a GPS antenna,

90 shaped like a giant mushroom, on the roof of the car. The antenna was connected to a laptop, upon which a map would show our progress—a GPS track. Singh took the wheel. Arcari sat in back with the laptop, ready to note any changes.

95 The first thing the men noticed was a "No Left Turn" sign out of the gas station. "That doesn't go in the database," Arcari said. "That's unofficial, since it pertains to a private enterprise."

An analyst has some leeway in proposing

100 research missions in his territory. "The situation at LaGuardia was something I had noticed myself and thought should be revisited," Arcari explained. In his free time, he'd been driving past the airport and, nudged by curiosity, if not

105 conscience, had made a little detour. He discovered that the Port Authority of New York

and New Jersey, which runs the airport, had put up a few new road signs.

"We'll circle around the perimeter and then

110 check the terminals," Arcari said. "As we're driving, I'm checking our information against what exists in reality." Left on Runway Drive ("drop a name check"), merge onto LaGuardia Road (another name check), left onto Delta

115 Arrivals Road. The sign for it was new. "A valid unnamed feature," Arcari said, turning the laptop so that I could follow along as he recorded it onscreen. "I point an arrow to where the feature occurred."

120 Seeing the road through the eyes of a ground-truther made it seem <u>a thicket of signage</u>—commands and designations vying for attention, like a nightmare you might have after a day of studying for a driving exam. Once you

125 start looking for **attributes**, you spot them everywhere.

"Why don't we loop around again?" Arcari said. "I want to be sure we collected everything correctly."

130 The familiar frustration of going around and around on an airport road was compensated for by the fact that no one was lost or late. After the extra <u>orbit</u>, we drove into a neighborhood next to the airport. Arcari approached the

135 neighborhood by driving around the outside of the "project area," and then going up and down the streets within it. He observed that, driving around like this, you become acutely aware of how many people are not at work. Arcari said

140 that one of the issues that has come up in New York in recent years is the naming of streets and squares for the victims of the attacks on September 11, 2001. We came upon one of them, James Marcel Cartier Way, and Arcari was

145 pleased to see that the name was in the database. A kind of contentment took hold, as other anomalies encountered along the way—an unlikely median strip, a "Do Not Enter" sign— turned out to be accounted for.

150 Over lunch at a local diner, we discussed various **attribute incidents.** "One **item** that was an issue: on the Brooklyn-Queens Expressway, they started renumbering the exits. They did some but didn't do others, so for a while there

155 were two Exit 41s."

After lunch, Arcari and Singh were due back at the central office, in Syosset, to download their findings. They offered to drive me back into Manhattan, but we agreed that it
160 would make more sense for me to take the subway. None of us knew where to find it, though. Subway stations are not **attributes**;

Navteq honors the automobile, a trend started by the makers of road maps of a century ago,
165 whose mandate was to promote auto travel and, with it, the purchase of gasoline, cars, and tires. We pulled into a gas station, and I ran inside to ask for directions. ■

**READING SKILL** | Identifying and Understanding Metaphors

**APPLY**

**A.** Think about the metaphors in Reading 1 and answer the questions in your notebook. Compare answers with a partner.

1. Line 16

   What is a *boiler room*? What does it mean to be "the boiler room" for an entire business?

2. Line 47

   What is a *blizzard*? Why does the writer choose this word to make his point?

3. Line 77

   What is a *thatch*? What does *mad* mean here? What is the author trying to communicate with this metaphor?

4. Line 121

   What is a *thicket*? Which other metaphor above is this one very similar to? What does it mean to *see something through someone else's eyes*?

5. Line 133

   What is an *orbit*? What image does this word suggest? Why does the writer use it in this context?

**B.** With a partner, read these metaphors and discuss them. Think of a context in which a writer might use them effectively. Share your ideas in a small group.

1. a sea of troubles: *The situation of a person who is ill, bankrupt, and lonely.*

2. a web of deceit: _____

3. a trail of lies: _____

4. a veil of secrecy: _____

5. a labyrinth of hallways: _____

An *attribute* is a quality or feature of someone or something.

> *They drive around and take note of what they call "**attributes**," anything of significance to a traveler seeking his way.*

The verb *attribute* means "to believe that something was caused or done by something or someone." It takes the preposition *to*. It can be used in active or passive form.

**Active:**  *He **attributed** his poor performance on the driving test to lack of sleep the night before.*

**Passive:**  *The fault for the accident **was attributed to** the driver of the other car.*

**Pronunciation note**: In the noun form, the stress is on the first syllable. In the verb form, the stress is on the second syllable.

CORPUS

**A.** Complete these sentences with the active or passive form of *attribute*. Be sure to use the correct tense. Read your completed sentences aloud to a partner, paying attention to pronunciation.

1. The guide _____ his excellent sense of direction to the years he spent with his grandfather, hunting and trapping in the woods.

2. The power failure on the east side of town _____ to the recent storms and high winds.

3. The map of the Texas interior _____ to Alonso de Santa Cruz.

4. He _____ her confidence on the road to the years she spent driving an ambulance in the city.

**B.** Put a check (✓) next to the things you think would be considered attributes by the ground-truthers in Reading 1. Discuss your answers in a small group.

___ 1. a stop sign

___ 2. an animal crossing area

___ 3. a mall's parking garage

___ 4. an automotive supply store

___ 5. a gas station

___ 6. a bus stop

___ 7. the poor condition of a major road

___ 8. a highway rest area

| Word Form Chart | | | |
|---|---|---|---|
| **Noun** | **Verb** | **Adjective** | **Adverb** |
| incident<br>incidence | _____ | incidental | incidentally |

The noun *incidence* generally refers to the number of times something (usually something bad) happens.

> There is a high **incidence** of traffic accidents during the first snowfall of the year.

The noun *incident* refers to a particular event, usually involving violence, danger, or something strange.

> There were two **incidents** of fighting among the fans at the football game.

The adjective *incidental* refers to minor events that accompany something bigger.

> Despite some **incidental** problems during construction, the building was completed on schedule.

The adverb *incidentally* is often used to change the subject, usually to something related but not very important. It has the same meaning as *by the way.*

> The mall was really crowded today, but I was able to find that sweatshirt for Peter. **Incidentally**, the travel bookstore you like isn't there anymore. It moved downtown.

CORPUS

**C.** In your notebook, restate each of these statements using the form of *incidence* given in parentheses.

1. The report on the radio said that there was a minor conflict at the soccer game last night, which caused the game to start a few minutes late. (*incident*)

   *The report on the radio said that an* **incident** *at the soccer game last night caused the game to start a few minutes late.*

2. In the general population, the rate of traffic accidents decreases in proportion to the age of the driver. (*incidence*)

3. The new Impressa has the highest safety rating of any car in its class from three major car-rating organizations—and it's the car that a lot of pop stars drive. (*incidentally*)

4. Before the guide started the tour of the presidential palace, she gave us some trivia about the buildings in the neighborhood. (*incidental*)

5. There was a strange event during the performance when the singer seemed to forget which song he was singing. (*incident*)

**D.** Circle the item that best completes each statement. In your notebook, write a few sentences explaining your choice. Be prepared to read your sentences aloud or discuss your ideas with the class.

1. For me, the closest equivalent to reading a book is...

   a. taking a nap.

   b. watching a movie.

   c. studying.

   d. listening to someone tell a story.

2. For me, the closest equivalent to playing with a small child is...

   a. writing an imaginative story.

   b. playing a sport.

   c. conducting a sociological experiment.

   d. watching a funny movie.

3. For me, the closest equivalent to an evening at the opera is...

   a. a visit to an art museum.

   b. a visit to the home of a relative I like.

   c. a visit to the home of a relative I don't like.

   d. going to a movie.

## Before You Read

Read these questions. Discuss your answers in a small group.

1. What is the difference between a dictionary and an encyclopedia? How is each one usually used?

2. What attributes might an online encyclopedia have that a printed book could not have?

3. If you were asked to write an encyclopedia entry on any subject, what would you choose? What types of information would you include? What would you exclude? What resources would you consult?

Whenever you use an encyclopedia for an academic paper, be sure to cite it as carefully as you would cite any other reference source. There are many encyclopedias on the Internet. Both printed and reputable online encyclopedias hire researchers and writers to supply their content.

**Caution**: One online encyclopedia, Wikipedia, relies on its *users* to provide content, who are not necessarily professional researchers. Anyone can write, edit, and update the entries on the website. For this reason, some instructors will not accept Wikipedia as a reference source for an academic paper, so check with your instructor before using it.

## 🔊 Read

**This entry from an online encyclopedia addresses navigation in the sense of determining position and direction on or above the surface of the Earth.**

# NAVIGATION

## METHODS

There are several different branches of navigation, including but not limited to the following. Click on terms to see individual entries:

- Celestial navigation—using observed positions of the sun, moon, stars, and sometimes planets to navigate at sea

5 - Pilotage—using visible natural and man-made features such as human-made sea marks and beacons, sometimes with the aid of a nautical **chart**, or map of marine and coastal areas

- Dead reckoning—using course and speed to determine position

- Off-course navigation—deliberately aiming to one side of the destination to allow for **variability** in the heading (direction)

10 - Electronic navigation—using electronic equipment such as radios and satellite navigation systems to follow a course; e.g., Electronic **Chart** Display and Information System (ECDIS), an electronic alternative to printed nautical **charts**

- Position fixing—determining current position by visual and electronic means

- Collision avoidance using radar

## HISTORY

15 Navigation is the science of accurately determining one's location and then planning and following a route. The earliest form of navigation was land navigation. This relied on physical landmarks to **chart** the journey from one place to 20 another. Away from land, one must use other markers in order to navigate successfully. One modern way to do this is to keep track of one's position using longitude and latitude. These are two kinds of imaginary lines drawn on maps or 25 globes representing the Earth. Latitude is distance north or south of Earth's equator. Longitude is distance east or west of the Greenwich Meridian, an imaginary line that runs from the North Pole to the South Pole and 30 through Greenwich, England.

Marine navigation may have begun when prehistoric people attempted to guide a vessel, perhaps a log, across the water using familiar coastal landmarks. In the pre-modern history of 35 human migration and nautical exploration, a few peoples have excelled as seafarers. Prominent examples include the Polynesians and the Micronesians of the Pacific Ocean.

The Polynesian navigators routinely crossed 40 thousands of miles of open ocean to reach tiny islands. They used only their own senses and knowledge of the sea that was passed down from generation to generation. In eastern

Polynesia, navigators memorized extensive catalogs
of information in order to help them navigate at
various times of day throughout the year. These
catalogs included the following kinds of information:
- The motion of specific stars, and where they
  would rise and set on the horizon of the ocean
- The weather
- Time of travel
- Wildlife species (some species **assembled** at
  particular locations)
- Ocean swells and how they would affect the crew
- The color of the sea and sky, especially how
  certain types of clouds would **assemble** at
  particular locations above some islands
- The angle at which navigators should approach
  a harbor

These sets of information were kept as *guild
secrets*. Generally, each island maintained a guild,
or group, of master navigators who had very high
status. In times of famine or difficulty, only they
could trade for aid or evacuate people. The guild
secrets were almost lost. Fortunately, one of the
last living navigators taught them to a professional
small-boat captain so that he could write them
down. The captain recorded these secrets in book
form, creating an early navigator's **manual**.

**The Big Dipper, Little Dipper, and North Star**

Ancient sailors used celestial bodies (that is,
objects in the night sky) to steer by. For example,
in the Northern Hemisphere one can look for the
constellation (group of stars) known in English as
the Big Dipper. Sailors could use the Big Dipper to
find the North Star, which tells which way is north.

But celestial navigation as it's known today
was not used until people better understood
the motions of the Earth, sun, and stars.
Nautical **charts** were developed to record new
navigational and piloting information for other
navigators. The development of accurate
celestial navigation allowed ships' crews to
better determine position.

The most important instrument for nautical
navigation was the navigator's diary. These
diaries contained **crucial** information. They
often became trade secrets because they
**enabled** safe travel to profitable ports.

One problem with all early forms of navigation
was that they required voyagers to be able to
see either land or sky. By the year 300, the
magnetic compass had been invented in
China. Sometime between 850 and 1050,
they became common navigational devices on
ships. Magnetic compasses allowed sailors to
continue sailing a course even when the
weather limited the sky's visibility. This
instrument also allowed the development of
dead reckoning. Dead reckoning can be used
to navigate when landmarks are out of sight,
although it still requires people to accurately
know their location from time to time.

Arab navigators in the 9th century developed a
celestial navigation tool called a *kamal*. A kamal
consists of a wooden rectangle and a length of
rope with evenly spaced knots. Navigators used
this instrument to measure the angle of a
particular star above the horizon, which allowed
a navigator to determine the ship's latitude.
Arab navigators were very successful with using
this device, establishing trade networks from
the Atlantic Ocean and Mediterranean Sea to
the Indian Ocean and China Sea. Navigators
from India and China later adopted use of the
kamal. A limitation of the kamal is that it's
mainly useful only in lower latitudes, or regions
relatively near the equator.

After Isaac Newton published the *Principia* in
1687, navigation was transformed. Mathematics
was applied to the study of nature, and the entire
world was measured using essentially modern
latitude instruments and the best available
clocks. In 1730, the sextant was invented.

A sextant uses mirrors to measure the altitude of celestial objects in relation to the horizon.

**Sextants have been used for centuries to navigate the sea.**

In the late 19th century, Nikola Tesla invented radio. Soon, radio beacons and radio direction finders were providing accurate land-based fixes,[1] even hundreds of miles from shore. This system lasted until modern satellite navigation systems made it obsolete.

Around 1960, LORAN was developed. This measured how long a radio wave took to travel between antennas at known locations. These measurements allowed travelers to fix positions. The equipment could then locate geographic positions to within a half mile (800 m). At about the same time, TRANSIT, the first satellite-based navigation system, was developed. It was the first electronic navigation system to provide global coverage.

In 1974, the first GPS satellite was launched. GPS systems now give accurate locations with an error of only a few meters. They also have **precision** timing, giving time measurements with an error of less than a microsecond (one millionth of a second). GLONASS is a positioning system that was launched by the Soviet Union. It relies on a slightly different model of the Earth. In 2007, the European Union approved financing to develop a competing system, named Galileo. China had some limited participation in developing Galileo, but in 2006 announced development of a GPS system of its own, to be named *Beidou*. *Beidou* is a Chinese name for the Big Dipper.

---

[1] *fixes*: determinations of one's exact location, usually made using radar, a known visual point, or astronomical observation

# Reading Comprehension

Mark each sentence as *T* (true) or *F* (false) according to the information in Reading 2. Use the dictionary to help you understand new words.

___ 1. Sailors using the method of celestial navigation might occasionally rely on the position of other planets for guidance.

___ 2. The most important item in the ancient navigator's toolbox was his diary.

___ 3. The sextant helped sailors more accurately determine their positions based on measuring the positions of the stars.

___ 4. The magnetic compass was recently invented by the European Union.

___ 5. Radio beacons and direction finders became obsolete after the invention of satellite navigation systems.

___ 6. Ancient Polynesian navigators crossed the open ocean with the aid of sophisticated clocks.

___ 7. Polynesian navigational knowledge passed down by oral tradition was finally written in book form.

___ 8. There are various navigation and positioning systems about which an online encyclopedia can provide information.

What sequence is described in the history of navigation? In your notebook, list at least six developments in this sequence, in order. Pay attention to time expressions such as *around the year 300* and adverbs of sequence such as *after* or *next*.

## Vocabulary Activities    STEP I: Word Level

A *chart* can take many forms. It can be a table, a graph, a diagram, or any graphic representation of information—for example, a Word Form Chart used in this book.

CORPUS

**A.** Match the picture of each chart with its type, listed in the box. Compare answers with a partner and discuss the function of each type of chart.

| | | |
|---|---|---|
| a. eye chart | c. flow chart | e. pie chart |
| b. flip chart | d. medical chart | f. sales chart |

___ 1.

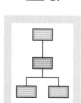

___ 2.

___ 3.

___ 4.

___ 5.

___ 6.

The word *precise* is an adjective meaning "clear and accurate; giving a lot of detail." The adverb form is *precisely* and has a similar meaning to *exactly.*

The noun form, *precision*, means "the quality of being clear or exact." *Precision* can also be used as an adjective to describe something that has precision.

> *Each and every component was manufactured with great **precision**.*
>
> *With **precision** tools, we can achieve more effective results with less cost.*

**B.** In your opinion, which of these items require precision? Put a check (✓) next to them. Why do you think it is crucial for them to be precise? Discuss your answers in a small group.

___ 1. measurements for new carpeting

___ 2. the time you agree to meet a friend

___ 3. a portrait (a painting of someone)

___ 4. a history book

___ 5. the fit of your clothes

___ 6. a legal agreement between two friends

___ 7. the position of items on your desk

___ 8. instructions to an experienced babysitter

*Vary* has many members in its word family. Here are example sentences to illustrate some of the more common ones. Check your dictionary for exact definitions.

**Nouns**

| | |
|---|---|
| variety | *Ancient travelers used a **variety** of landmarks to navigate their way.* |
| variation | *Most coastal cultures developed the canoe, but there are many **variations** in its design.* |
| variance | *His conclusions were totally at **variance** with the evidence.* |
| variable | *New car designers consider **variables** like where it will be driven, weather conditions, and how many passengers it might carry.* |

**Adjectives**

| | |
|---|---|
| various | *There are **various** routes you can take to get to work, but this is the fastest.* |
| variable | *Be careful driving here at night. Road conditions are **variable** and sometimes dangerous.* |

CORPUS

**C.** Complete these sentences using a form of *vary.*

1. Some people _____ their routes depending on the day and time.

2. Engine temperature is the most important _____ to pay attention to when driving in the desert.

3. He decided to move to California for _____ reasons.

4. Reports from the different field offices were at _____ with our expectations.

5. The GPS system in the rental car had a wide _____ of options for customizing our itinerary.

6. Researchers have found wide _____ in driving ability among people of _____ ages.

**D.** Complete the sentences about another type of information system. Use each target vocabulary term once. Compare answers with a partner.

| | | | |
|---|---|---|---|
| assemble | crucial | items | prohibit |
| attribute | enable | manual | significant |
| chart | equivalent | precisely | |

1. The Aboriginal people of Australia had a system of songs, called the Songlines. These songs identified landmarks and other _____ (things) (plants, rocks, waterholes) useful in finding one's way through the desert.

2. The Songlines were _____ (identical) to a continental navigational _____ (map) , or a kind of Australian travel _____ (instruction book) .

3. In addition to describing the physical _____ (characteristics) of each _____ (important) landmark, the songs also often explained how the landmarks were created and named.

4. Aboriginals used this labyrinth of pathways to _____ (come together) for rituals, to _____ (allow) or _____ (not allow) travel across territorial boundaries, or to hunt for food and water.

5. To work well as a navigational system, it was _____ (extremely important) that the songs be sung in the appropriate order and that each song be sung _____ (exactly right) .

As an adjective or adverb, *manual* or *manually* means "done by the hands."

> *Building a road requires a lot of machines, but also a lot of **manual** labor.*
>
> *When the power went out, we had to do everything **manually**.*

As a noun, a *manual* is a book that explains how to do or operate something.

> *I can't figure out how to fix this. I need a **manual**.*

CORPUS

**E.** In your notebook, write a short description of these items. Explain who might use each one and for what purpose. Discuss your ideas with a partner.

1. an owner's (or user's) manual
2. a writer's style manual
3. a computer manual
4. a wilderness survival manual
5. a camera manual

*Crucial* can be used as a simple adjective before the noun, as in a *crucial decision*. To make the meaning stronger or more dramatic, use an "it" sructure.

> *It is **crucial** that she get to the hospital within the hour.*

Notice the grammar in the above sentence: . . . *crucial that she get* . . . . This grammar is common in sentences with "it" structures that stress importance or urgency.

> *It's important <u>that</u> he know the truth.*
>
> *It is vital <u>that</u> it get finished today.*

CORPUS

**F.** Write one or more answers for each of these questions. Discuss your answers in a small group. Decide which of your ideas is the most crucial in each case. Discuss your choices with the class.

1. What is a crucial problem for humanity?

   *Environmental pollution poses a crucial problem for humanity.*

2. What was a crucial moment in history?

   _____

3. What is a crucial decision you must make for your future?

   _____

4. What is one piece of crucial information needed for navigating at sea?

   _____

**G.** Read these situations. In your notebook, explain what must be done in each case, using the word in parentheses. Try to use the grammar noted in the box above. Be prepared to read your sentences aloud or discuss them with the class.

1. You have a test in the morning that will make up 50 percent of your grade. (*crucial*)

   *It is crucial that you get a good night's sleep before the test.*

2. You have gotten three speeding tickets this year. If you get one more, your license will be taken away. (*important*)

3. Your elderly grandmother is arriving on a plane at 2 p.m., but you have to work until 3 p.m. Your friend has volunteered to pick her up for you. (*essential*)

4. You found exactly the car you want after months of looking. Three other people want it, too. The owner has promised it to you, if you give her the money for it today. (*vital*)

5. Your little nephew's birthday party is tomorrow morning. You bought him a special toy he has wanted for a long time, and now you have to assemble it. It has many small parts and a ten-page instruction manual. (*necessary*)

**H.** Self-Assessment Review: Go back to page 145 and reassess your knowledge of the target vocabulary. How has your understanding of the words changed? What words do you feel most comfortable with now?

## Writing and Discussion Topics

Write about or discuss the following topics.

1. Plan a trip around the world. From your city, make precisely ten stops before you return. In charting your course, try to make the most efficient use of time and money. How long will the trip take? How will you get from city to city? What will you do in each place? How will you get around?

2. What predictions would you make for the future of navigation? Have we advanced as far as we can in this field? Is there anything missing that you would like to see someday?

3. Think carefully about all the navigational attributes you rely on in your daily travels for school, work, shopping, or socializing. Which of these attributes do you consider to be the most crucial?

# The Academic Word List

**Words targeted in Level 3 are bold**

| Word | Sublist | Location |
|------|---------|----------|
| abandon | 8 | L1, U7 |
| **abstract** | **6** | **L3, U5** |
| **academy** | **5** | **L3, U1** |
| access | 4 | L1, U2 |
| accommodate | 9 | L2, U7 |
| accompany | 8 | L1, U2 |
| accumulate | 8 | L2, U4 |
| accurate | 6 | L4, U6; L0, U2 |
| achieve | 2 | L4, U1; L0, U9 |
| acknowledge | 6 | L1, U7 |
| acquire | 2 | L1, U4 |
| adapt | 7 | L4, U7 |
| adequate | 4 | L2, U4 |
| adjacent | 10 | L2, U3 |
| adjust | 5 | L4, U3 |
| administrate | 2 | L1, U3 |
| **adult** | **7** | **L3, U6** |
| advocate | 7 | L1, U10 |
| affect | 2 | L2, U6; L0, U10 |
| aggregate | 6 | L1, U9 |
| aid | 7 | L2, U7 |
| albeit | 10 | L1, U7 |
| allocate | 6 | L2, U6 |
| alter | 5 | L1, U1 |
| alternative | 3 | L1, U10 |
| ambiguous | 8 | L1, U4 |
| amend | 5 | L2, U9 |
| analogy | 9 | L1, U4 |
| analyze | 1 | L2, U3; L0, U01 |
| annual | 4 | L1, U9 |
| anticipate | 9 | L2, U3 |
| apparent | 4 | L2, U9 |
| append | 8 | L2, U10 |
| **appreciate** | **8** | **L3, U5** |
| **approach** | **1** | **L3, U1; L0, U10** |
| appropriate | 2 | L1, U8 |
| **approximate** | **4** | **L3, U4** |
| arbitrary | 8 | L2, U8 |
| area | 1 | L4, U1; L0, U5 |
| **aspect** | **2** | **L3, U4** |
| **assemble** | **10** | **L3, U10** |
| assess | 1 | L1, U8 |
| assign | 6 | L2, U9 |
| assist | 2 | L2, U5; L0, U4 |
| assume | 1 | L2, U1; L0, U4 |
| **assure** | **9** | **L3, U4** |
| **attach** | **6** | **L3, U7** |

| Word | Sublist | Location |
|------|---------|----------|
| attain | 9 | L1, U5 |
| attitude | 4 | L4, U6 |
| **attribute** | **4** | **L3, U10** |
| author | 6 | L2, U4 |
| authority | 1 | L1, U6 |
| **automate** | **8** | **L3, U6; L0, U7** |
| **available** | **1** | **L3, U5; L0, U6** |
| aware | 5 | L1, U5 |
| **behalf** | **9** | **L3, U9** |
| benefit | 1 | L4, U2; L0, U9 |
| bias | 8 | L4, U8 |
| bond | 6 | L4, U3 |
| **brief** | **6** | **L3, U6** |
| bulk | 9 | L4, U9 |
| capable | 6 | L1, U8 |
| capacity | 5 | L4, U9 |
| category | 2 | L4, U5 |
| cease | 9 | L4, U10 |
| **challenge** | **5** | **L3, U8** |
| channel | 7 | L1, U3 |
| **chapter** | **2** | **L3, U7** |
| **chart** | **8** | **L3, U10** |
| chemical | 7 | L2, U10 |
| circumstance | 3 | L2, U10; L0, U8 |
| cite | 6 | L4, U10 |
| civil | 4 | L1, U4 |
| clarify | 8 | L4, U8 |
| **classic** | **7** | **L3, U9** |
| clause | 5 | L2, U8 |
| code | 4 | L4, U9 |
| coherent | 9 | L2, U5 |
| coincide | 9 | L1, U5 |
| collapse | 10 | L4, U10 |
| colleague | 10 | L1, U5 |
| **commence** | **9** | **L3, U9** |
| **comment** | **3** | **L3, U3** |
| **commission** | **2** | **L3, U9** |
| commit | 4 | L2, U6; L0, U8 |
| commodity | 8 | L4, U6 |
| **communicate** | **4** | **L3, U2** |
| community | 2 | L2, U7; L0, U4 |
| compatible | 9 | L1, U9 |
| **compensate** | **3** | **L3, U4** |
| compile | 10 | L2, U6 |
| complement | 8 | L1, U7 |

| Word | Sublist | Location |
|------|---------|----------|
| complex | 2 | L4, U2; L0, U1 |
| component | 3 | L4, U3 |
| compound | 5 | L4, U6 |
| comprehensive | 7 | L2, U7 |
| comprise | 7 | L4, U9 |
| compute | 2 | L4, U8 |
| conceive | 10 | L4, U10 |
| **concentrate** | **4** | **L3, U8** |
| **concept** | **1** | **L3, U1; L0, U10** |
| conclude | 2 | L1, U6 |
| concurrent | 9 | L4, U5 |
| conduct | 2 | L1, U9 |
| confer | 4 | L4, U4 |
| confine | 9 | L1, U10 |
| confirm | 7 | L4, U10 |
| conflict | 5 | L1, U2 |
| conform | 8 | L4, U7 |
| consent | 3 | L4, U7 |
| consequent | 2 | L2, U3; L0, U4 |
| **considerable** | **3** | **L3, U8** |
| consist | 1 | L4, U2, U9; L0, U7 |
| constant | 3 | L4, U8 |
| constitute | 1 | L1, U4 |
| constrain | 3 | L1, U8 |
| **construct** | **2** | **L3, U1; L0, U5** |
| consult | 5 | L1, U6 |
| consume | 2 | L2, U2; L0, U10 |
| contact | 5 | L2, U10 |
| contemporary | 8 | L1, U7 |
| context | 1 | L1, U4 |
| **contract** | **1** | **L3, U9** |
| contradict | 8 | L2, U2 |
| contrary | 7 | L1, U6 |
| contrast | 4 | L1, U7 |
| contribute | 3 | L1, U9 |
| controversy | 9 | L2, U3 |
| convene | 3 | L1, U4 |
| converse | 9 | L2, U8 |
| convert | 7 | L2, U2 |
| convince | 10 | L1, U3 |
| cooperate | 6 | L1, U2 |
| coordinate | 3 | L2, U6 |
| core | 3 | L2, U5 |
| corporate | 3 | L2, U2 |
| **correspond** | **3** | **L3, U9** |
| **couple** | **7** | **L3, U1** |
| create | 1 | L2, U1; L0, U1 |

| Word | Sublist | Location |
|------|---------|----------|
| 🔑 **credit** | 2 | **L3, U6** |
| 🔑 **criteria** | 3 | **L3, U3** |
| 🔑 **crucial** | 8 | **L3, U10** |
| 🔑 culture | 2 | L4, U10; L0, U6 |
| **currency** | 8 | **L3, U9** |
| 🔑 cycle | 4 | L4, U5 |
| | | |
| 🔑 data | 1 | L2, U3; L0, U10 |
| 🔑 debate | 4 | L2, U4 |
| 🔑 decade | 7 | L1, U7 |
| 🔑 decline | 5 | L1, U2 |
| deduce | 3 | L4, U7 |
| 🔑 **define** | 1 | **L3, U2; L0, U4** |
| 🔑 **definite** | 7 | **L3, U4** |
| 🔑 demonstrate | 3 | L1, U5 |
| denote | 8 | L4, U6 |
| 🔑 deny | 7 | L4, U10 |
| 🔑 depress | 10 | L2, U4 |
| 🔑 derive | 1 | L4, U10; L0, U10 |
| 🔑 design | 2 | L1, U1; L0, U5 |
| 🔑 **despite** | 4 | **L3, U2** |
| detect | 8 | L1, U6 |
| deviate | 8 | L2, U8 |
| 🔑 device | 9 | L2, U3 |
| 🔑 **devote** | 9 | **L3, U9** |
| differentiate | 7 | L1, U4 |
| dimension | 4 | L4, U5 |
| diminish | 9 | L4, U4 |
| discrete | 5 | L2, U6 |
| discriminate | 6 | L1, U10 |
| displace | 8 | L2, U7 |
| 🔑 **display** | 6 | **L3, U5; L0, U8** |
| dispose | 7 | L4, U6 |
| **distinct** | 2 | **L3, U7** |
| **distort** | 9 | **L3, U6** |
| 🔑 distribute | 1 | L4, U8 |
| diverse | 6 | L2, U8 |
| 🔑 document | 3 | L4, U9 |
| domain | 6 | L2, U8 |
| 🔑 domestic | 4 | L1, U3 |
| 🔑 dominate | 3 | L1, U5 |
| 🔑 **draft** | 5 | **L3, U6** |
| 🔑 **drama** | 8 | **L3, U5** |
| duration | 9 | L4, U1 |
| dynamic | 7 | L1, U5 |
| | | |
| 🔑 economy | 1 | L1, U7 |
| edit | 6 | L4, U8 |
| 🔑 element | 2 | L4, U1 |
| 🔑 eliminate | 7 | L2, U9 |
| 🔑 emerge | 4 | L2, U1 |

| Word | Sublist | Location |
|------|---------|----------|
| 🔑 emphasis | 3 | L2, U9 |
| **empirical** | 7 | **L3, U4** |
| 🔑 **enable** | 5 | **L3, U10** |
| 🔑 **encounter** | 10 | **L3, U5** |
| 🔑 energy | 5 | L2, U5 |
| enforce | 5 | L4, U7 |
| **enhance** | 6 | **L3, U1** |
| 🔑 **enormous** | 10 | **L3, U8** |
| 🔑 ensure | 3 | L2, U5; L0, U6 |
| entity | 5 | L4, U5 |
| 🔑 **environment** | 1 | **L2, U1; L3, U8; L0, U3** |
| equate | 2 | L2, U2 |
| equip | 7 | L2, U3 |
| 🔑 **equivalent** | 5 | **L3, U10** |
| erode | 9 | L1, U9 |
| 🔑 error | 4 | L1, U10 |
| 🔑 establish | 1 | L1, U6 |
| 🔑 estate | 6 | L4, U6 |
| 🔑 estimate | 1 | L2, U10 |
| ethic | 9 | L2, U9 |
| 🔑 **ethnic** | 4 | **L3, U3** |
| evaluate | 2 | L1, U10 |
| eventual | 8 | L4, U3 |
| evident | 1 | L4, U2; L0, U8 |
| evolve | 5 | L2, U7 |
| exceed | 6 | L4, U1 |
| 🔑 exclude | 3 | L4, U7 |
| 🔑 exhibit | 8 | L2, U5 |
| 🔑 expand | 5 | L1, U7 |
| 🔑 **expert** | 6 | **L3, U8** |
| explicit | 6 | L1, U3 |
| exploit | 8 | L1, U5 |
| 🔑 export | 1 | L1, U3 |
| 🔑 **expose** | 5 | **L3, U5** |
| external | 5 | L2, U10 |
| **extract** | 7 | **L3, U2** |
| | | |
| facilitate | 5 | L4, U1 |
| 🔑 **factor** | 1 | **L3, U8; L0, U4** |
| 🔑 feature | 2 | L4, U1; L0, U2 |
| 🔑 federal | 6 | L2, U3 |
| 🔑 fee | 6 | L1, U1 |
| 🔑 file | 7 | L4, U6 |
| 🔑 final | 2 | L4, U3 |
| 🔑 finance | 1 | L2, U2 |
| finite | 7 | L1, U9 |
| **flexible** | 6 | **L3, U9** |
| fluctuate | 8 | L2, U7 |
| 🔑 **focus** | 2 | **L3, U8** |
| format | 9 | L4, U8 |

| Word | Sublist | Location |
|------|---------|----------|
| 🔑 formula | 1 | L4, U8 |
| forthcoming | 10 | L4, U3 |
| 🔑 found | 9 | L4, U8 |
| 🔑 foundation | 7 | L4, U4 |
| framework | 3 | L1, U1 |
| 🔑 **function** | 1 | **L3, U1** |
| 🔑 **fund** | 3 | **L3, U3** |
| 🔑 fundamental | 5 | L4, U4 |
| furthermore | 6 | L4, U9 |
| | | |
| gender | 6 | L2, U8 |
| 🔑 generate | 5 | L1, U5 |
| 🔑 generation | 5 | L1, U7 |
| **globe** | 7 | **L3, U2** |
| 🔑 **goal** | 4 | **L3, U3** |
| 🔑 grade | 7 | L1, U7 |
| 🔑 grant | 4 | L2, U9 |
| 🔑 guarantee | 7 | L2, U8 |
| **guideline** | 8 | **L3, U3** |
| | | |
| **hence** | 4 | **L3, U5** |
| **hierarchy** | 7 | **L3, U4** |
| 🔑 highlight | 8 | L4, U3 |
| hypothesis | 4 | L4, U7 |
| | | |
| identical | 7 | L4, U5 |
| 🔑 identify | 1 | L4, U2; L0, U7 |
| ideology | 7 | L4, U6 |
| ignorance | 6 | L2, U9 |
| 🔑 illustrate | 3 | L4, U9 |
| 🔑 **image** | 5 | **L3, U5** |
| immigrate | 3 | L2, U1 |
| 🔑 impact | 2 | L1, U9 |
| implement | 4 | L1, U2 |
| implicate | 4 | L4, U7 |
| implicit | 8 | L1, U3 |
| 🔑 imply | 3 | L4, U7 |
| 🔑 impose | 4 | L1, U10 |
| incentive | 6 | L1, U10 |
| **incidence** | 6 | **L3, U10** |
| incline | 10 | L1, U7 |
| 🔑 income | 1 | L1, U3 |
| incorporate | 6 | L4, U4 |
| 🔑 index | 6 | L1, U4 |
| 🔑 indicate | 1 | L2, U4; L0, U10 |
| 🔑 individual | 1 | L1, U1 |
| **induce** | 8 | **L3, U7** |
| 🔑 inevitable | 8 | L2, U8 |
| infer | 7 | L1, U8 |
| infrastructure | 8 | L4, U6 |
| inherent | 9 | L1, U1 |

🔑 Oxford 3000™ words

| Word | Sublist | Location | Word | Sublist | Location | Word | Sublist | Location |
|------|---------|----------|------|---------|----------|------|---------|----------|
| inhibit | 6 | L1, U5 | major | 1 | L3, U2; L0, U5 | overseas | 6 | L1, U1 |
| initial | 3 | L3, U7; L0, U8 | manipulate | 8 | L4, U4 | | | |
| initiate | 6 | L2, U10 | manual | 9 | L3, U10 | panel | 10 | L1, U6 |
| injure | 2 | L1, U1 | margin | 5 | L4, U3 | paradigm | 7 | L2, U6 |
| innovate | 7 | L1, U3 | mature | 9 | L1, U8 | paragraph | 8 | L3, U6 |
| input | 6 | L3, U6 | maximize | 3 | L2, U8 | parallel | 4 | L3, U9 |
| insert | 7 | L2, U9 | mechanism | 4 | L3, U9 | parameter | 4 | L4, U5 |
| insight | 9 | L3, U7 | media | 7 | L1, U5 | participate | 2 | L1, U8 |
| inspect | 8 | L3, U3 | mediate | 9 | L4, U2 | partner | 3 | L3, U1 |
| instance | 3 | L1, U6 | medical | 5 | L1, U2 | passive | 9 | L2, U8 |
| institute | 2 | L2, U8 | medium | 9 | L2, U2 | perceive | 2 | L2, U9 |
| instruct | 6 | L4, U2 | mental | 5 | L2, U6 | percent | 1 | L2, U10 |
| integral | 9 | L1, U4 | method | 1 | L4, U9 | period | 1 | L2, U6 |
| integrate | 4 | L2, U7 | migrate | 6 | L3, U2 | persist | 10 | L2, U4 |
| integrity | 10 | L3, U7 | military | 9 | L1, U4 | perspective | 5 | L3, U2 |
| intelligence | 6 | L3, U8 | minimal | 9 | L2, U10 | phase | 4 | L1, U8 |
| intense | 8 | L1, U2 | minimize | 8 | L1, U1 | phenomenon | 7 | L2, U5 |
| interact | 3 | L1, U8 | minimum | 6 | L4, U5 | philosophy | 3 | L4, U5 |
| intermediate | 9 | L2, U7 | ministry | 6 | L1, U2 | physical | 3 | L4, U4; L0, U4 |
| internal | 4 | L3, U7 | minor | 3 | L3, U7 | plus | 8 | L4, U5 |
| interpret | 1 | L3, U3 | mode | 7 | L4, U7 | policy | 1 | L3, U3 |
| interval | 6 | L2, U5 | modify | 5 | L2, U3 | portion | 9 | L3, U9 |
| intervene | 7 | L2, U8 | monitor | 5 | L2, U3 | pose | 10 | L3, U1 |
| intrinsic | 10 | L4, U4 | motive | 6 | L1, U6 | positive | 2 | L1, U5 |
| invest | 2 | L2, U4 | mutual | 9 | L3, U3 | potential | 2 | L4, U8; L0, U10 |
| investigate | 4 | L4, U8 | | | | practitioner | 8 | L1, U2 |
| invoke | 10 | L1, U3 | negate | 3 | L4, U2 | precede | 6 | L2, U4 |
| involve | 1 | L2, U3 | network | 5 | L3, U2 | precise | 5 | L3, U10 |
| isolate | 7 | L3, U4 | neutral | 6 | L2, U10 | predict | 4 | L2, U1 |
| issue | 1 | L4, U2; L0, U8 | nevertheless | 6 | L4, U10 | predominant | 8 | L1, U8 |
| item | 2 | L3, U10; L0, U7 | nonetheless | 10 | L4, U7 | preliminary | 9 | L4, U1 |
| | | | norm | 9 | L4, U6 | presume | 6 | L2, U2 |
| job | 4 | L1, U1 | normal | 2 | L3, U8 | previous | 2 | L2, U5; L0, U5 |
| journal | 2 | L2, U6 | notion | 5 | L4, U9 | primary | 2 | L1, U1 |
| justify | 3 | L2, U3 | notwithstanding | 10 | L2, U1 | prime | 5 | L4, U4 |
| | | | nuclear | 8 | L2, U7 | principal | 4 | L4, U5 |
| label | 4 | L2, U2 | | | | principle | 1 | L3, U9; L0, U9 |
| labor | 1 | L1, U2 | objective | 5 | L1, U10 | prior | 4 | L3, U6 |
| layer | 3 | L3, U4 | obtain | 2 | L3, U6; L0, U10 | priority | 7 | L1, U2 |
| lecture | 6 | L4, U2 | obvious | 4 | L3, U7 | proceed | 1 | L4, U9; L0, U3 |
| legal | 1 | L2, U3 | occupy | 4 | L1, U9 | process | 1 | L1, U9 |
| legislate | 1 | L3, U3 | occur | 1 | L1, U2 | professional | 4 | L1, U5 |
| levy | 10 | L2, U9 | odd | 10 | L1, U8 | prohibit | 7 | L3, U10 |
| liberal | 5 | L2, U1 | offset | 8 | L4, U8 | project | 4 | L4, U4,U9 |
| license | 5 | L3, U9 | ongoing | 10 | L3, U3 | promote | 4 | L2, U6 |
| likewise | 10 | L4, U5 | option | 4 | L4, U7 | proportion | 3 | L1, U10 |
| link | 3 | L1, U8; L0, U1 | orient | 5 | L2, U5 | prospect | 8 | L2, U6 |
| locate | 3 | L2, U1; L0, U1 | outcome | 3 | L3, U4 | protocol | 9 | L2, U4 |
| logic | 5 | L1, U6 | output | 4 | L1, U7 | psychology | 5 | L4, U2 |
| | | | overall | 4 | L2, U6 | publication | 7 | L3, U1 |
| maintain | 2 | L4, U1; L0, U9 | overlap | 9 | L1, U7 | publish | 3 | L1, U3 |

Oxford 3000™ words

| Word | Sublist | Location | Word | Sublist | Location | Word | Sublist | Location |
|---|---|---|---|---|---|---|---|---|
| 🔑 purchase | 2 | L2, U9; L0, U7 | 🔑 secure | 2 | L4, U6; L0, U8 | terminate | 8 | L1, U9 |
| 🔑 **pursue** | **5** | **L3, U8** | 🔑 seek | 2 | L4, U3; L0, U4 | 🔑 text | 2 | L2, U4 |
| | | | 🔑 **select** | **2** | **L3, U1** | 🔑 theme | 8 | L2, U2 |
| **qualitative** | **9** | **L3, U9** | **sequence** | **3** | **L3, U5** | 🔑 theory | 1 | L4, U4; L0, U9 |
| 🔑 quote | 7 | L4, U10 | 🔑 **series** | **4** | **L3, U5** | thereby | 8 | L4, U3 |
| | | | 🔑 sex | 3 | L1, U3 | thesis | 7 | L4, U7 |
| **radical** | **8** | **L3, U4** | 🔑 shift | 3 | L4, U9; L0, U2 | 🔑 **topic** | **7** | **L3, U3** |
| random | 8 | L2, U7 | 🔑 **significant** | **1** | **L3, U10; L0, U6** | 🔑 trace | 6 | L1, U9 |
| 🔑 **range** | **2** | **L3, U1** | 🔑 similar | 1 | L2, U1; L0, U2 | 🔑 **tradition** | **2** | **L3, U6; L0, U4** |
| 🔑 ratio | 5 | L1, U8 | **simulate** | **7** | **L3, U1** | 🔑 transfer | 2 | L4, U1; L0, U3 |
| **rational** | **6** | **L3, U3** | 🔑 site | 2 | L1, U6 | 🔑 transform | 6 | L2, U7 |
| 🔑 react | 3 | L2, U6; L0, U3 | so-called | 10 | L2, U8 | **transit** | **5** | **L3, U5** |
| 🔑 **recover** | **6** | **L3, U4** | sole | 7 | L4, U1 | transmit | 7 | L4, U4 |
| refine | 9 | L4, U4 | 🔑 somewhat | 7 | L1, U4 | 🔑 transport | 6 | L4, U10; L0, U9 |
| regime | 4 | L2, U10 | 🔑 **source** | **1** | **L3, U2; L0, U10** | 🔑 trend | 5 | L4, U6 |
| 🔑 **region** | **2** | **L3, U1** | 🔑 specific | 1 | L1, U6 | **trigger** | **9** | **L3, U7** |
| 🔑 register | 3 | L2, U2 | specify | 3 | L4, U6 | | | |
| **regulate** | **2** | **L3, U6; L0, U9** | **sphere** | **9** | **L3, U7** | 🔑 ultimate | 7 | L1, U9 |
| reinforce | 8 | L2, U5 | 🔑 stable | 5 | L4, U5 | undergo | 10 | L4, U1 |
| 🔑 reject | 5 | L1, U7 | statistic | 4 | L4, U7 | underlie | 6 | L4, U6 |
| 🔑 relax | 9 | L1, U8 | 🔑 **status** | **4** | **L3, U2** | undertake | 4 | L2, U3 |
| 🔑 release | 7 | L4, U1 | **straightforward** | **10** | **L3, U4** | 🔑 **uniform** | **8** | **L3, U1** |
| 🔑 relevant | 2 | L4, U8 | 🔑 strategy | 2 | L2, U5; L0, U9 | unify | 9 | L4, U5 |
| reluctance | 10 | L2, U4 | 🔑 stress | 4 | L4, U4 | 🔑 unique | 7 | L2, U1; L0, U7 |
| 🔑 **rely** | **3** | **L3, U2; L0, U6** | 🔑 structure | 1 | L2, U1; L0, U5 | **utilize** | **6** | **L3, U8** |
| 🔑 **remove** | **3** | **L3, U2; L0, U8** | 🔑 style | 5 | L1, U4 | | | |
| 🔑 require | 1 | L4, U2; L0, U9 | submit | 7 | L2, U9 | 🔑 valid | 3 | L4, U10 |
| 🔑 research | 1 | L4, U2 | subordinate | 9 | L4, U3 | 🔑 **vary** | **1** | **L3, U10; L0, U2** |
| reside | 2 | L1, U2 | subsequent | 4 | L1, U1 | 🔑 vehicle | 8 | L4, U3 |
| 🔑 **resolve** | **4** | **L3, U4** | subsidy | 6 | L2, U2 | 🔑 **version** | **5** | **L3, U5** |
| 🔑 **resource** | **2** | **L3, U8** | 🔑 substitute | 5 | L1, U1 | 🔑 via | 8 | L1, U4 |
| 🔑 respond | 1 | L4, U7 | successor | 7 | L2, U9 | **violate** | **9** | **L3, U6** |
| 🔑 **restore** | **8** | **L3, U5** | 🔑 sufficient | 3 | L2, U10; L0, U4 | virtual | 8 | L2, U10 |
| restrain | 9 | L2, U7 | 🔑 sum | 4 | L1, U10 | 🔑 **visible** | **7** | **L3, U5** |
| 🔑 restrict | 2 | L2, U9; L0, U6 | 🔑 summary | 4 | L2, U10 | 🔑 vision | 9 | L4, U3 |
| 🔑 retain | 4 | L4, U3 | supplement | 9 | L4, U10 | **visual** | **8** | **L3, U7** |
| 🔑 **reveal** | **6** | **L3, U8** | 🔑 survey | 2 | L1, U3 | 🔑 volume | 3 | L2, U4 |
| revenue | 5 | L2, U2 | 🔑 **survive** | **7** | **L3, U2** | voluntary | 7 | L1, U10 |
| 🔑 reverse | 7 | L2, U7 | suspend | 9 | L1, U10 | | | |
| 🔑 **revise** | **8** | **L3, U6** | sustain | 5 | L2, U4 | welfare | 5 | L4, U1 |
| 🔑 revolution | 9 | L1, U1 | 🔑 symbol | 5 | L2, U2 | 🔑 whereas | 5 | L4, U2 |
| rigid | 9 | L2, U7 | | | | whereby | 10 | L1, U4 |
| 🔑 role | 1 | L1, U5 | 🔑 tape | 6 | L1, U6 | widespread | 8 | L4, U10 |
| 🔑 route | 9 | L2, U5 | 🔑 **target** | **5** | **L3, U10** | | | |
| | | | 🔑 task | 3 | L1, U8 | | | |
| **scenario** | **9** | **L3, U7** | 🔑 team | 9 | L2, U6 | | | |
| 🔑 schedule | 8 | L4, U9 | 🔑 technical | 3 | L1, U6 | | | |
| scheme | 3 | L4, U3 | 🔑 technique | 3 | L2, U1; L0, U6 | | | |
| scope | 6 | L4, U8 | 🔑 **technology** | **3** | **L3, U8; L0, U7** | | | |
| 🔑 section | 1 | L2, U5 | 🔑 temporary | 9 | L1, U9 | | | |
| 🔑 sector | 1 | L1, U3 | tense | 8 | L1, U10 | | | |

🔑 Oxford 3000™ words